japanamerica

To Tayla:
Ganbatte kudasai!

japanamerica

How Japanese Pop Culture Has Invaded the U.S.

roland kelts

palgrave
macmillan

JAPANAMERICA

First published in hardcover in 2006 by
PALGRAVE MACMILLAN™
175 Fifth Avenue, New York, N.Y. 10010 and
Houndmills, Basingstoke, Hampshire, England RG21 6XS
Companies and representatives throughout the world.

PALGRAVE MACMILLAN is the global academic imprint of the Palgrave Macmillan division of St. Martin's Press, LLC and of Palgrave Macmillan Ltd. Macmillan® is a registered trademark in the United States, United Kingdom and other countries. Palgrave is a registered trademark in the European Union and other countries.

ISBN-13: 978–1–4039–8476–0 paperback
ISBN-10: 1–4039–8476–X paperback

Library of Congress Cataloging-in-Publication Data

Kelts, Roland.
    Japanamerica : how Japanese pop culture has invaded the U.S. / by Roland Kelts.
        p. cm.
    Includes bibliographical references and index.
    ISBN 1–4039–7475–6 (hard cover)
    1. Popular culture—United States—Japanese influences.
2. United States—Civilization—1970– 3. Popular culture—Japan.
4. Japan—Civilization—1945– I. Title. II. Title: Japan America.

E169.12.K46 2006
303.48′27305209045—dc22   2006049109

A catalogue record for this book is available from the British Library.

Design by Newgen Imaging Systems (P) Ltd., Chennai, India.

First PALGRAVE MACMILLAN paperback edition: November 2007

10 9 8 7 6 5 4

Printed in the United States of America.

*For my family on both sides of
the world*

The whole of Japan is a pure invention.
There is no such country, there are no such people.
—Oscar Wilde

contents

acknowledgments

This book would not exist without the contributions of British writer and journalist Leo Lewis, who shared in the interviewing, researching, creating, compiling and editing of its pages. To him, I offer my deepest bow.

Lisa Kato, Kyoko Onoki and Mika Whitehurst are professional translators who were invaluable in parsing the nuances of the Japanese language, both during real-time interviews and in reviewing the text. Several low bows to each, and to Nahoko Araki, who helped arrange many of my visits with anime producers.

Many professionals on both sides of the world granted me their time and expertise. In the United States, Susan Napier, Charles Solomon and Frederik L. Schodt deserve deep bows. In Japan, Yoshihiro Shimizu, Masakazu Kubo and Hideki Ono and many others deserve the same. In particular, I lower my head to the tatami for Eiko Tanaka, president and founder of Studio4C and one of the few women producing anime, for sharing her knowledge and her network of fellow producers and publishers.

Michael Arias and Steve Alpert, rare Americans working inside the Japanese anime industry, gave me guided tours of their respective studios, and offered penetrating, cross-cultural insights. Shunsuke Narutani and Renfield Kuroda helped me navigate Akihabara, anime's nerve center in Tokyo.

At Palgrave, my deep thanks to Airie Stuart for giving me this opportunity, to Toby Wahl for precise and empathetic editing, and to the entire team for their patience and faith.

japanamerica

foreword

A few years ago I flew from New York to Los Angeles to visit some friends and conduct an interview for a story I was writing. I had recently flown from Tokyo to New York, and Japan was fresh on my mind.

At the time, my friends, a husband and wife with a four-year-old daughter, lived in Los Angeles' Echo Park neighborhood. The area was gentrifying fast: hipsters and artists were moving in, rents were rising, cafés were cropping up on corners and side streets. We walked with their daughter in nearby Elysian Park, where you can see both the Los Angeles skyline and Dodger Stadium.

Their house had a Japanese look and feel to it—smooth wood surfaces, subdued hues, straight lines; set back from the street on a hill, and obscured from view by a bank of shrubs and a bamboo grove. But the Japanese look and feel was purely coincidental. Urbane and highly educated professionals, my friends were planning to move into a new home shortly. Neither of them has a Japanese background, or any other reason to be focused on the culture. This house was a temporary landing pad.

One evening I sat in the living room with their daughter, watching the setting sun through the bamboo stalks beyond the window. Suddenly she began to cry. Her parents were rushing to prepare dinner in the kitchen and dining room behind us. I tried to console her myself, making silly faces and asking her about one of her dolls. I failed. Soon she was wailing, and I felt helpless.

Her mother swept gracefully into the room, calm as a mother, voice hushed and soothing. Some version of there, there, honey is what she said. Then: "Do you want to watch *Totoro*?"

I thought that I misheard her, but it was not the appropriate time to ask an intrusive question. When director Hayao Miyazaki's densely verdant countryside filled their widescreen TV, I knew that I had not.

Their daughter was entranced, leaning forward on the sofa, eyes wide as the tears dried on her cheeks, her mouth a slack oval. Miyazaki's plucky sisters and persevering, bushy-haired father came into view, and she uh-ohed and then giggled along with them, uttering some of the lines in unison with the animated figures on the screen.

3

"It's the only thing that settles her down when she's really upset," my friend explained, shrugging. "She absolutely loves *Totoro*. And we do, too."

I used to tell my American friends that America seemed surprisingly close to me whenever I stayed in Japan, even before high-speed Internet access went from being a luxury to being a necessity. The Japanese media is notably America-centered, partly because U.S. military bases still occupy enormous plots of an already crowded archipelago, and partly because America has a position as role model for the postwar generation. The Japanese who had survived the bombs and heard their Emperor declare defeat sought to rise from the ashes of World War II—and saw in their former conqueror possibilities for material and social wealth and well-being.

American fast-food restaurants and brand names are omnipresent in Japan's urban centers. With slightly less buzz and fanfare, a growing number of mainstream Hollywood movies open on or near their premieres in America, and CDs by American or English artists are sometimes even released earlier in Japan, where enormous Tower Records or HMV outlets prominently feature them, along with massive back catalogs.

In fact, until the deeper linguistic and cultural differences between the Japanese and other nationals become apparent, it is not uncommon to detect a tone of faint disappointment in the voices of first-time visitors, visitors who have landed expecting and hoping for something more exotic.

I used to say that Japan seemed very distant whenever I returned to the United States. American newscasts are generally focused on the fifty states, venturing overseas only for wars, natural disasters, or to dog the president with questions about foreign affairs. The occasional story about a foreign culture's quirky traditions might appear near the end of a newscast, but international stories of any stripe—and especially those about a land as far from U.S. shores as Japan—generally receive short shrift. The Nikkei rose or fell; a typhoon tore through Tokyo. That's about it.

But that has begun to change. And I began to notice the shift in the early years of this century. There is still an enormous imbalance of attention, of course. America dominates the global discourse for reasons good and bad, in positive and (increasingly) negative ways. But since that evening in L.A., I have started seeing a lot more copies of *My Neighbor Totoro* and other Miyazaki films in American friends' living rooms, and also seeing more Pokemon figures on the sides of buses, more *Akira* posters on college campuses, and more Japanese or Japanese-influenced titles of all types on American television. Though I am naturally more sensitive to them, references to Japan as having a cool or attractive culture are not likely to surprise anyone in twenty-first-century America.

The questions are: Why Japan? And why now?

Japanamerica is an attempt to explore the answers. It is not exclusively focused on Japanese *manga* (graphic print narratives) or anime—a word that is a Japanese truncation of the English word "animation" and is applied to all animated images in Japan, but only to Japanese animation in America—nor is it an attempt to analyze, explain, or serve as a guide for the two related media. There are now shelves of other books and print magazines that handle those tasks brilliantly and exhaustively, written by experts, academics, journalists, and aficionados from both countries, not to mention a fast-expanding range of Web sites, blogs, and Web publications created by devotees young and old.

Instead, I have set out to discover the reasons behind what many cultural historians are calling a third wave of Japanophilia—outsiders' infatuation with Japan's cultural character. The first wave occurred in the eighteenth and nineteenth centuries, when European artists discovered a uniquely Japanese aesthetic, and the second in the late 1950s and early 1960s, when beatnik writers and poets were drawn to Japan's ascetic spiritual traditions.

But what is unique about the current wave is the very modern, even futuristic, nature of the Japanese culture being sought. There are always some Americans interested in iconic totems of Japanese culture, like the *bushido* samurai tradition that emphasizes honor and discipline, *ikebana* flower arrangements, tea ceremonies, and Zen.

Now, however, it is the eccentricities, spastic zaniness, and libertarian fearlessness of Japan's creators of popular culture—and of the mind-bendingly acquisitive Japanese consumers of that culture—that are attracting the attention of Americans. These Americans may eventually develop a keenness for calligraphy or sumo, but anime and manga are at the cutting edge.

The story line of Sophia Coppola's 2003 film *Lost in Translation*, as well as the film's box office success, offers useful insights into the Japanamerica phenomenon. From the outset, the film is obsessed with contemporary Japan, from panning shots of Tokyo's animated and vivid neon signs to the electric energy of its flashing and bleeping arcade-riddled side streets; from the sleek, minimalist designs of Tokyo's modern hotels and sushi counters to the hum of its streaming crowds, escalators, and trains; from far-out fashions to funky partiers and DJs; from strip clubs to karaoke.

When Charlotte, the female lead, takes the bullet train to Kyoto, the shots of traditional Japanese icons—temples and shrines, gardens with pools of carp, a Shinto wedding procession—feel almost obligatory, as if we are being reoriented with reminders of our more conventional images of Japan before we plunge back into the kinetic prism of modern Tokyo.

The film's popularity is partly the result of the performances of its actors and the skills of its creators, of course. But the story was not set in just any foreign city, or in just any Asian one. Professional reviews and casual responses uttered at dinner and cocktail parties prominently mentioned Tokyo, as well as Japan. As in Woody Allen's films and their renderings of New York, in *Lost in Translation* the city became one of the star attractions. And suddenly, everyone I knew wanted to visit.

The majority of the material in this book is the result of interviews conducted in the United States and in Japan from March 2003 to the spring of 2006, with some exceptions. I spoke to Nigo, Japan's hip-hop fashion guru, twice: once in 2002 and once in 2004. And I have interviewed Haruki Murakami, Japan's most internationally famous and critically acclaimed contemporary novelist, several times since 2000, most recently in 2005.

Most of the interviews were done through personal, one-on-one conversations; some were conducted by phone, and a few, most significantly with the American author Frederik Schodt, were by necessity done through email. When others' writings are paraphrased or quoted, they are cited directly in my text.

I cast a wide net. For me, Japan is not merely a hip Asian nation blipping on American radar screens. It is also my mother's homeland, home to several of my closest relatives and dearest friends, and the land that has taught me more about my own native land, America, than I could ever have imagined when I first moved to Japan as an adult. It is a personal, more than a professional, obligation for me to tell a true story in these pages.

The book tries to adhere to some sense of chronology, but writing about the dense web of interrelations between America and Japan is too complex for a "once upon a time" framework. Instead, I take an approach more akin to manga or anime: I view the story from many angles, many perspectives, to find the thread of awareness that has been sewn into a greater fabric.

A few examples: Many Americans find in anime a vision of the future, a fresh way of telling stories and interpreting the world. Many Japanese, even within the industries that produce the art, are stunned that Americans care about their products. (No one in America is surprised that foreigners like our popular or mass culture.) From the Japanese perspective, they have been making and consuming anime for decades: What's the big deal?

Also, Americans I spoke to tend to assume that most Japanese anime artists and their producers are becoming rich. Not so, at least not yet.

And finally: Japanese over forty still care deeply about what Americans think of them. But younger Japanese do not blink. They strut through their cities with a confidence that borders on punk, and Americans like me are decidedly off their radar screens.

Japanamerica attempts to tell you why this is happening. If you wonder why your kids are more taken by Totoro than mesmerized by Mickey, or if you think *The Matrix* and *Kill Bill* arrived out of nowhere, this book is for you. Thanks to the Internet, nonstop flights, and restless new generations, Japan is a lot closer to America than ever before.

Last year, a friend in New York sent me a link to a Manhattan Internet dating portal. On it, an exasperated male's blurb was featured on the front page: "If you can't or won't eat sushi—don't even think about getting a date in NYC."

That is Japanamerica.

1
may the g-force be with you

In April 1977, the American television producer Sandy Frank attended the MIP-TV (Marché International de Programmes) conference in Cannes, France, an annual event that began in 1963 as an adjunct to the famous Cannes film festival. The MIP-TV conference continues to attract international television professionals, distributors, and broadcasters seeking access to new content, with a recent focus on the Internet licensing trade. Thirty years ago, of course, there was no Internet, no DVD or VCR, no TiVo. Television had established itself as the single dominant form of communication and entertainment in the American home, and it could largely rely on a captive, stationary audience. Programming for the then limited, real-time hours of peak viewership was a demanding if heady business: Get it right, and you reach (and might make) millions.

Frank was a rising star. A year earlier, the NYU graduate and former NBC staffer had become the first television distributor to have three prime-time, first-run syndicated TV shows on the air at the same time: *The New Name That Tune*, *The New Treasure Hunt*, and *The Bobby Vinton Show*. His earlier packaged distribution deals included *The Lone Ranger*, *Lassie*, and *The Bill Cosby Show*.

Given the range of his successes, it is hard to deny Frank's instinctive understanding of what Americans like to watch. His emphasis on variety and game shows presaged the contemporary flowering of Oprah Winfrey, *American Idol*, and numerous reality shows. But his place in the American pop culture pantheon took a dramatic twist that April at Cannes.

It was the year that Tatsunoko Production Co., Ltd., a small Japanese animation producer run by the three Yoshida brothers from Kyoto, had traveled to Cannes for their first international showcase, buoyed by the minor overseas success of the stylish animated series *Mach Go Go Go*, known to English speakers as *Speed Racer*. *Speed Racer* had proven to be a draw with teenagers (mostly boys) in an after-school time slot. While the Yoshidas knew that America was a tough market for Japanese animation—largely owing to hidebound American perceptions of animation as children's fare—they finally had a title that they thought they could sell to a new generation.

11

In their homeland it was called *Kagaku ninja-tai Gatchaman*, and it had already proven wildly successful on Japanese television. Its story and characters boasted fundamentals that spoke directly to Japan's cultural values: the "hero" is in fact a team, whose members must rely upon one another and not stand out as individuals; while there are distinct villains, a sense of evil tends to permeate the atmosphere, as though evil could emerge from anywhere, even from within the flawed and sometimes selfish heroes themselves; the ramifications of war are tragic (the father of one of the characters dies); and the heroes' ultimate mission, to defend the earth from complete annihilation and restore peace and stability, justifies their need to fight.

In short, *Gatchaman* emanated from the imaginations of what the artist Takashi Murakami now calls the world's first postapocalyptic society—the offspring of two atomic bombs, whose subterranean traumas, he believes, force them to see the world anew, and whose vision is best expressed through the underground and censor-free media of manga and anime.

But when Sandy Frank, a New Yorker, encountered the sharp lines, elaborate and intricate plot twists, and evocative yet recognizable settings, he saw mythic potential. "It was unlike anything else on American TV at the time—which of course was its problem," he remembers. "It was not only new and unproven; it was also not produced in America." Not to mention that *Gatchaman* also featured violence, blood, death, sexual innuendos, and morally questionable and sometimes visibly mortal heroes— which could all be found in the more daring and sophisticated American cinema of the 1970s, of course, but not in what mainstream Americans called cartoons.

A month later, on May 25, 1977, a science fiction, outer-space movie named *Star Wars* was released in theaters throughout the United States. Its rapid and widespread success marked Hollywood's first use of the term "blockbuster," and its subsequent product tie-ins, spin-offs, and sequels transformed the industry's approach to both marketing and mythmaking. Media producers scrambled to capitalize, scouring the United States for similarly sophisticated sci-fi storylines and equally arresting graphics.

But Sandy Frank thought of that April in Cannes, and of *Gatchaman*, and he immediately penned a letter to the Yoshida brothers in Tokyo. "I just thought to myself: 'With *Gatchaman*, I'm looking at *Star Wars*. I'm looking at an animated version of *Star Wars*.' It just blew me away."

the meta-mystery

Japan has undergone one of the most rapid evolutions of any foreign nation in the American psyche—and at warp speed. As a child of mixed parentage (my father is American, my mother Japanese), I have been unusually and sometimes uncomfortably close to an international relationship almost blissfully rooted in ignorance, or at least willful misunderstanding.

In my lifetime, Japan has gone from the vanquished World War II foe (with lingering connotations of "sneaky backstabber" from the attack on Pearl Harbor) that rose from the ashes to churn out cheap copycat goods, like the electric guitars that my bandmates and I ridiculed as teenagers, to manufacturing automatons (group-think competitors in the electronics and automotive sectors) in the 1980s, to the rich and reliably peaceful economic ally of recent decades. *America and the Four Japans*, by translator and manga specialist Frederik L. Schodt, takes a thorough look at this elaborate role-playing dance.

But it was back in 1977 that Frank, motivated by the unexpected success of *Star Wars*, sought Japan's contemporary cultural output—the nation's imagination—in the form of an animation series for import to the United States. So enamored were he and his colleagues of the seemingly endless reach of *Star Wars*, they immediately rebranded the Japanese animation, *Battle of the Planets*.

For Frank, a lot more than editing would be necessary to sell Americans on his foreign find. With no Japanese translators at the ready, and an untested overseas genre on his hands, much more grafting, cutting, rewriting, inserting, twisting, and tweaking would be required to draw the nods of network censors and a whole host of heartland affiliates and sponsors.

"I totally revisioned the whole thing," he says now. "We had the cartoons themselves and the Japanese scripts and we totally redid the whole series. We did new music, new scenes—we even invented a new character that looked like R2-D2. We had 7-Zark-7 there to smooth over all the rough spots in the plot. There was an antiviolence campaign in the U.S. at that time, so we had to take out most of the violence, and there was a lot of it in the original. There was death and blood, and it had to go. We took it out— much to my regret, of course. Twenty years later, violence was back in and we could have cleaned up with the same series."

Frank's team attempted a western whitewashing of the darker undercurrents in Japanese animation: No one died, plot points were softened by the R2-D2 clone, anomie was replaced by logic, or at least some signs of cause and effect, and the entire series was moved to a distant planet to avoid earthly unpleasantness. Frank's staff could neither read nor understand Japanese, so they spent painstaking hours in the studio matching English words to the mouth movements of the cartoon characters. They interpreted the plots visually and replaced the quirky-sounding Japanese tunes with America-friendly soundtracks.

The result? Aside from *Godzilla* features on late night TV, a disfigured, hosed-down but still breathing *Battle of the Planets* became America's first major encounter with a new style of Japanese pop culture. And by 1979, Frank says, "we had it running on 100 network affiliates throughout the U.S., from 4 to 6:30, Monday to Friday." In other words, they had a hit. For many American teens and young adults, this would be their first taste of Japanese pop. Some of them got hooked for life. But even thirty years ago, many sensed that what they saw in blazing anime color on their NBC affiliates was not the whole picture, which made the show even more compelling. It added another layer of narrative intrigue to the show itself, a kind of meta-mystery for young viewers: What are they hiding from us? What have they changed?

"I watched *Battle of the Planets* regularly, and I knew even at a young age that something was really weird," recalls Lawrence Eng, who holds a doctorate in American *otaku* (geek, or obsessive fan) studies from New York's Rensselaer Polytechnic Institute. "I think most of us knew that the American version was different, but we didn't even know for sure where the original came from. We just knew it looked cool."

Battle of the Planets was certainly no more advanced in production values than other animations on American TV at the time. If anything, it was more primitive. The action was jerky, the movements sometimes oddly out of sync, the drawings sometimes disproportionate, as when characters shrank too quickly in size as they receded into the distance, entering absurdly tall elevators or doorways drawn onto unchanging (and so money-saving) backgrounds.

Sometimes the low-budget atmosphere itself was a source of fascination. I remember watching *Battle* and other titles, such as *Speed Racer* and *Star Blazers*, with a neighborhood pal. Every so often one of us would point a finger at an odd facial expression or out-of-sync bit of dialogue. Highlighting, then mocking an error with laughter provided comic relief from the seriousness of the story lines. It also provided us preteens with the chance to feel momentarily superior to shows that nevertheless sucked us back in every school day afternoon.

The characters looked different and fresh. The animation sometimes emphasized the racier parts of the human body. Their modes of transport had sleek yet believable shapes. And when the characters fought, they didn't just zap one another, as in most American cartoons. They grappled, hand to hand.

Adding to the visual titillation was the fact that each character was defined by personal dilemmas, tics, and shortcomings that made them feel more complex and less predictable. If they were not more real, perhaps, then at least they were more engaging, especially to North American kids raised on the slapstick gags and one-note portrayals (When will that stupid coyote ever learn?) that dominated standard network animation.

"There was this lack of direct confrontation in most U.S. stuff at the time," recalls Thomas Lee, a Canadian who moved to Japan in pursuit of his passion for anime, and now runs his own Tokyo-based English school. He remains an avid anime fan and, he confesses with solemnity, a recovered video game addict. Like Eng and others I spoke to, Lee is in his early thirties, part of the first-generation wave of anime fans with indelible childhood memories of *Speed Racer* and *Battle of the Planets*.

"The American stuff was frustrating. You'd have shows like the *A-Team* or *Superman*, with these powerful heroes. And then, they'd just wind up shooting at walls or lifting heavy objects. Or else you'd just see Tom and Jerry wrapping their bodies around chairs or getting hit in the head with pans. But think of Japanese shows like *Ultraman Taro* or *Power Rangers*. Those guys really kick ass."

Lee also remembers his love of anime's outlines and edges. "American cartoons had soft, round figures. There was a stronger reality to the anime, a vividness, even down to the controls on the spaceship, which really looked real and corresponded to very specific actions. Even though I knew *Battle* had been edited, I saw those details and was hooked."

anime style is everywhere

Thirty years later, Japan's hip twenty-first century incarnation is itself a hit in America. No longer seen as the manufacturing king of Asia (a crown China is bearing unsteadily), Japan is now the region's most visible arbiter of cool, via video and computer games, postmodern pop music trends, cuisine, clothing, mix-'n'-match light-speed fashion scenes and, especially, its iconic animations and graphic novels.

There were earlier signs of Japan's identity shift, to be sure. The recent evolution of sushi in the American psyche and palate, from an exotic threat to a grocery store mainstay, is among the most obvious and revealing ones.

Sushi is not merely raw fish, raw being un-American, and fish being relatively low on Americans' list of carnivorous preferences. It is also an entire *style* of eating that until quite recently felt alien to most of us. Technically, you can use a fork, spoon, and knife to eat almost all other Asian (or ethnic) cuisines, from Chinese fare to pad thai. But try using them on your sushi. In addition to physically destroying the food itself, you are likely to receive several quizzical, or downright nasty glares—not merely from the wait staff and chefs, but also from your fellow Americans. Sushi helped make chopsticks inevitable; chopsticks have become unremarkable, an infiltration of American life.

On the side of pop culture, although the Power Rangers and Pokemon phenomena predate this century, it is not by much. The former is filled with the confrontational violence and hand-to-hand grappling that drew the young Thomas Lee and others to the bowdlerized *Battle* series in the late 1970s, and its mass success bolsters Frank's lament that his brainchild was born twenty years too early.

But the gargantuan success of Pokemon is, like sushi, singularly revealing, partly owing to the ubiquity of Pikachu, the series' bright yellow, moon-eyed mascot. Unlike Disney icons such as Mickey, Donald, Dumbo, or Nemo, a mouse, duck, elephant, and clown fish, respectively, or Hanna Barbera's Yogi Bear, Pikachu is an animated representation of precisely nothing we know in our physical world, introducing Americans to just one aspect of Japanese pop culture's creative freedom. And while the Belgian-born *Smurfs* series presented Americans with similar animated inscrutability throughout the '80s (prompting a character in Richard Linklater's 1991 debut, *Slacker*, to crack: "What the hell is a smurf, anyway?"), Pikachu is but one of 395 different species, all of them fictional. Loosed from the gravity of realism, or even of a more finite fictional world, Pokemon's producers have been able to create what is now known as the multibillion dollar Pokemon media franchise: video games, anime, manga—and the series's ever-proliferating trading cards.

In April 2006, Tsunekazu Ishihara, the president of Pokemon Co., explained a decade of American success to the *Nikkei Shimbun*, Japan's *Wall Street Journal*, in precisely those terms. "The basic concept of Pokemon games has remained unchanged since the first release in 1996. But we have always strived to add new characters and upgrade games so that Pokemon fans will never feel they are approaching an end. That is the reason for the prolonged popularity. We're set to release more new characters by the end of this year, bringing the total number to slightly less than 400."

As a foreign-born infiltrator of American culture, and probably to the chagrin of at least some parents, Pokemon leaves Smurfdom in the dust.

If the signs of a rising Japanamerica were visible in earlier years, the twenty-first century has seen what has become a veritable surge of contemporary Japanese culture in the American psyche.

In a 2002 article for the *New Yorker* magazine, writer Rebecca Mead, citing the fast-paced creative energy, visual inventiveness, and acquisitive consumer intensity of its contemporary culture, announced that Tokyo had superseded Paris as the world's fashion capital. She also noted that few Japanese designers bothered invading the West with their wares, focusing for economic reasons on nearby markets in Asia.

Mead's proof was A Bathing Ape, the uber-cool, retro anime-style imprint of a thirty-something designer, entrepreneur, and DJ who calls himself Nigo, and who sells his products—mostly street wear like T-shirts, jackets, jeans, and sneakers—in tightly controlled, limited editions.

Look again. Nigo now operates stores in the heart of London's Carnaby Street trend zone and in the center of Soho in New York. He partnered with Pepsi a few years ago to design cans and other merchandise (again, limited edition), and more recently he forged a creative alliance with half-Japanese American hip-hop star and mutual admirer Pharell Williams. Together, Nigo and Williams launched a transnational designer label, Billionaire Boys Club. Williams's new CDs, released worldwide, are designed by Bathing Ape.

When I met Nigo on a couple of occasions in the basement showroom of his offices and studios in central Tokyo, I asked him how he accounted for the spike in Americans' interest in contemporary Japanese culture. His answer was a shrug: "Ten or fifteen years ago, the previous generation was happy just purchasing goods from the U.S. or Europe. The influence was moving mostly in one direction. But my generation wants to be the creative center now. We want to make what's new right here in Tokyo, and we want to spread it to the world."

As Nigo was returning his influences in the worlds of hip-hop and fashion (his first designer wear was an imitation of the down jackets adorning the members of '80s rappers, Run DMC), another twenty-first-century anime-style infiltration, the virtual band, Gorillaz, in which each member is an anime character, began appearing on U.S. pop charts. Their most popular music video, all done in Japanese-style animation, contains a stunning visual denouement lifted directly from director Hayao Miyazaki's *Castle in the Sky*—the film that inspired Gorillaz's British illustrator, Jamie Hewlett.

Their virtual lead guitarist is a tiny Osaka-born Japanese teenage girl character named "Noodle," who allegedly arrived straight from Japan in a FedEx box. (Noodle's voice is that of actress Haruki Kuroda, who hosted a kid's video gaming show named *PXG*.) Gorillaz debuted on prime-time U.S. television in the opening performance of the 2006 Grammy Awards show— sharing the stage with one of America's most physical and flesh-oriented superstars, Madonna. Another long-standing tradition in Japanese popular culture (and one I long thought would never work in the U.S. or U.K.)—hit-producing music stars that are known only as animated characters—has invaded the American mainstream.

Other flesh-and-blood MTV rock and pop stars are boarding the anime bandwagon, most notably Linkin Park, whose 2004 hit song and animated music video, *Breaking the Habit*, was produced by Tokyo's GDH productions and transformed into a manga by importer TokyoPop. The copious amount of animation, Japanese or anime influenced, featured on MTV and other youth-targeted cable channels is a good barometer of how comfortable the next generations are with the medium.

In its generally august (or dryly parochial, depending on your passion for bookish Manhattanites) publishing industry pages, the *New York Times* reported in the winter of 2006 that manga represents one of the few quantifiable growth sectors of the U.S. publishing industry. A month later, in March, TokyoPop, one of two major importers of manga to America, inked a distribution and publishing partnership with HarperCollins. The other major importer, Viz Media, had expanded its own distribution relationship with Simon & Schuster at the beginning of the year. Attendance at New York City's first large-scale comics convention that same month, the New York Comic-con, featuring numerous manga titles, so far exceeded expectations that organizers were forced to turn away hundreds of advance ticket holders—and city fire marshals were called in to the Javits Center to turn away thousands more clamoring to get in.

American publishers, desperate for growth of any kind, are paying close attention. The word out of major book fairs in London, Paris, and New York is that book buyers are scrambling en masse to the manga booths and displays—first to find out what it is, then to start selling it.

America's skyrocketing interest in anime, manga's kinetic cousin, over the past few years is equally striking. The Anime Network, a cable channel showing only Japanese titles, 24/7, debuted in 2002, promising viewers "the newest and hottest shows, directly from Japan" in the breathy tones of a bootlegger trafficking in contraband. Recent estimates of anime video and DVD sales peg the U.S. figure at half a billion dollars; no one dares speculate on the numbers for ancillaries such as TV, merchandising, and licensing profits for toys, games, and related paraphernalia. More than a dozen U.S. channels, both network and cable, regularly broadcast anime titles. One U.S. animation industry executive estimates that the anime business is growing so fast—surpassing its own projections annually—that no one can really keep track of it.

But it is not just the anime or manga titles themselves that have Americans engaging a culture thousands of miles across the Pacific. What we might call anime style permeates nearly every feature on the face of Japan's contemporary image. We are as familiar today with the hollow-eyed, mouthless look of a Hello Kitty doll, or a Pokemon or Yu-Gi-Oh card, as we are with Mickey, Donald, and the golden arches. Last summer, while waiting in line at a tiny country store in rural Maine, I encountered Yu-Gi-Oh's spiky blond head and half-moon purple pupils glaring at me from a placard near the cash register—above a handwritten cardboard sign reading: "Live bait for sale."

New York's Macy's Thanksgiving Day Parade in 2005 featured Puffy AmiYumi, a Japanese female pop duo who now have legions of young American fans solely because their anime likenesses appear daily in a series on the Cartoon Network. Their pop careers having flashed and fizzled over a decade ago at home, the two singers became the first Japanese to have their own float in one of America's few entirely indigenous holiday events.

In advertisements on the same network broadcasting the parade, Geico, one of America's largest car insurance companies, bombarded viewers with a campaign featuring a clip (rescripted, of course) from the Yoshida brothers' forty-year-old *Speed Racer* series. The ad featured the main character, Trixie, his girlfriend, and Chim-Chim, the chimpanzee sidekick. It's a knowing, insider wink to the U.S. demographic whose first glimpse of anime-style graphics now means that they're in the prime of their car-insurance-buying lives.

In the wake of the hypersuccessful *Matrix* series, which was directly and openly indebted to several anime films in particular and to the style in general, and of Hayao Miyazaki's 2003 animation Oscar for *Spirited Away*, Hollywood is embracing anime as primary source material. Remakes of *Akira* and *Evangelion*, two international classics, have long been in the works. *Crouching Tiger*'s Billy Kong has signed on to make a live-action version of *Blood: The Last Vampire*. *Titanic* mega-director James Cameron is creating two films based on the anime *Battle Angel Alita*, due for release in 2007 and 2008, and allegedly combining animation, live action, and 3-D computer-generated images (CGI). And action-hero/*Pulp Fiction* hipster Samuel L. Jackson is the voice of *Afro Samurai*. The series, produced in Japan by Tokyo's GDH Productions, is now running on Spike TV. Next year it will become a mixed anime/live-action feature film, in which Jackson will star. Even *Astro Boy*, the first proper anime series by the father of the genre, Osamu Tezuka, is reportedly being made into a live-action film.

And those are just the direct descendents of anime style. The *New York Times* recently proclaimed that Japanese food was where French cuisine stood in the 1950s—poised to enter the mainstream—with a new Japanese restaurant cropping up on Manhattan street corners nearly every week. Like sushi, most Japanese cuisine is partly a visual feast—colorfully laid out on lacquer ware or multicolored plates, and, if fresh, visibly prepared by knife-wielding chefs with warriorlike precision and speed.

And how about Toyota's "Prius"—a brand name that could be the atavistic title of an anime film or character name—for a futuristic car that runs partly on electricity, as if by magic, or in a manga?

Why has anime style, the feel and aura of a very specific, still relatively homogeneous culture thousands of miles away, suddenly become so appealing to us? Americans are not seeking British, French, Korean, or Chinese cartoon graphics or cartoon-style cultural images in large numbers. After selling us cars and electronics, have the Japanese begun to give the American people what we want in other forms, applying their now globally acknowledged ingenuity and work ethic to attracting America's tastes in entertainment?

Of all foreign nationals, the Japanese, in particular, owing to their years under U.S. occupation, can draw upon decades of American pop iconography to decipher the psyche of their former conqueror. But it is the very Japaneseness of the anime, manga, and cultural icons that American fans and critics seek—not direct mimics of our own aesthetic styles.

it is america that has changed

I was raised in America. Having visited Japan as a child and teenager, and lived in Tokyo and Osaka for several years as an adult, I often marvel that the gap between America and Japan is not wider. For Americans, Japan's cultural norms can seem not only alien, but virtually opposite to our own. The Japanese value restraint, conformity, and consent. We prize self-assertion, individuality, and iconoclasm. They tend to be meticulous and obsessed with perfecting the minute; we produce blockbusters and build Hummers. Japan is an archipelago of confined spaces, and its strict social formalities have evolved to help millions survive in them. America has big skies, vast plains, easy smiles, and hearty pats on the back.

Japan really is different from America, and in some respects, radically so. But, paradoxically, the strict codes of etiquette and behavior that govern daily life in Japan also allow for an extraordinary degree of creative and social permissiveness—the freedom to explore other identities, to test the limits of possibility.

It does not hurt that Japanese crime rates remain so low. Both women and men can stroll through the streets of Tokyo, the world's most populous city, late into the night, having just disposed of legions of assassins at a video arcade, or romanced a handsome but dangerous tycoon at a manga *kissa* (comics café), or dressed up as an anime warrior at a *cosplay* (costume play) event, or belted out their favorite karaoke tunes in the persona of their favorite pop star—all while safe in the knowledge that, after their indulgences, they are not in danger. The excitement, eroticism, thrill-seeking, and violence—the very thrills of our imaginations— are unlikely to greet you unexpectedly in Japan, in physical form, on your way home.

It is this creative freedom, something that we cherish in the United States as a cultural touchstone, that is at least partly behind the most innovative characteristics of Japanese popular culture: the little white kitty famously composed of seventeen lines, four colors, and no mouth whose appeal transcends global boundaries; the fuzzy yellow Pikachu; the numerous manga and anime, some of which explore physical transformation, philosophical conundrums, and dense personal trauma with daring visuals and unexpected plot turns. You may be a staid Japanese businessman by day, but at night and on weekends, the culture lets you craft your own identity. A virtual after-hours self.

We are all becoming better acquainted with our virtual selves, especially through the Internet, where chat rooms, blogs, and other modes of immediately gratifying communication offer the possibility for virtual transformation, for a freedom beyond conventional boundaries. As this happens, of course, the split between who we are or must be publicly, and who we yearn to be and sometimes are in private, may grow deeper.

But in Japan, there are two very specific words to define these selves: *tatemae*, or the presentation of your public self, and *honne*, how you really feel. The underlying truth.

"It's America that has changed, not Japan," says Yoshiro Katsuoka, a planning director for Marvelous Entertainment, one of Japan's most active anime and video game producers. He is exercising his flair for the provocative, eyebrows dancing, voice rising, but he is also addressing a deeper shift: Japanese companies no longer need to localize their pop culture products, at least not to the same extent that they have in the past, to appeal to American audiences. Even the manga that is translated into English today retains certain Japanese phrases and writing in the native characters—undecipherable and illegible to most U.S. readers, but still considered cool.

"When *Gatchaman / Battle of the Planets* went to the U.S., it was bent to suit American tastes," Katsuoka says. "But the weird thing is that now American tastes have been bent to be more Japanese." Even as privacy laws are being tested in America, by Internet crime and the U.S. government, among others, and maybe in reaction to those disappearing boundaries, he believes that Americans are more avidly cultivating their private fantasies, pursuing their personal obsessions, deepening the divide between their public and their other selves. Becoming, in short, American otaku.

"People say we in Japan are the *tatemae* society, that everything we say and do is merely on the surface and acts as a screen for our real thoughts and desires. But America is the true *tatemae* society! Puritanism is just *tatemae*. And," he adds, "so is the myth of a happy ending."

another kind of ending

The idea that the Japanese were postmodern before the term was coined has been floated for many years now by journalists, academics, and artists, most of whom cite similar characteristics: their smorgasbord of global cultural borrowings, first from Asia, then from Europe and America, with little regard for origins or authenticity; their comfort with (and sometimes preference for) simulations and simulacra; their apparently easy and seamless coexistence with high-tech gadgetry and ancient ritual; their blurring of lines between high and low culture, good and evil, the self and the other; and their intensely visual culture, which dates back centuries.

To anyone who has stayed in Japan longer than a tourist, however, it is clear that some of the above claims are absurd. The necessary use of honorifics in the language when you are speaking to your superiors is but one of many examples in which clear distinctions and rigid hierarchies remain firmly intact. The lines between high and low art may not be as explicit in a Japanese department store art exhibition as they are in the Met or the Louvre, but as writer Ian Buruma and others have noted, artistic definitions of the serious and the unserious have long held sway in Japan, and still do today.

In fact, Buruma reminded Americans of that point in an essay he wrote in the *New York Review of Books*, responding to the theories of artist Murakami, who produced an exhibition on Japanese pop culture for New York's Japan Society in the summer of 2005. The exhibition itself was a Japanese-style smorgasbord, spanning everything from the international lizard antihero, Godzilla, to domestic Japanese animated TV icons like Doraemon, with only brief explanations of the logic behind the choices.

Murakami's theories about the origins of manga and anime were more detailed, if not always academically sound: The dropping of the atomic bombs created a trauma in Japanese culture for which there was no precedent in world history. Publicly at least, and perhaps sensing no other option, the majority of

Japanese wanted to forget their post-traumatic stresses and move forward quickly (very postmodern, very Japanese). Established artists, working in the realm of *tatemae*, the public self in the public discourse, largely chose not to address their society's post-traumatic stress disorder (PTSD)—anxieties, fears, rages, and other emotional turmoil—engendered by the bombs.

According to Murakami, only manga and anime artists and their otaku brethren could do so, and they did. They were working on a lower cultural frequency, in the realm of *honne*, or real feeling, and so they were free to express what they (and others) actually felt. They were not only free to do so, they were expected to.

Thus, Murakami surmises, Japan became the first truly postapocalyptic society. And Japanese anime and manga—and by extension, its popular or low culture—were the first expressions of what a certain kind of brave, new world truly feels, looks, and acts like.

The title of Murakami's show was *Little Boy*, one of the two names assigned to the atomic bombs by the U.S. military, a phrase Murakami also applies to Japan's embrace of a diminutive role in its relationship to its American conqueror. The original title of Japan's first major manga, created in the early 1960s by Tezuka, the widely acknowledged father/inventor of what has become anime style, is *The Mighty Atom*, which became *Astro Boy* in the U.S.

Though not entirely new, and though greeted by accusations of oversimplicity and a list of exceptions, what is interesting about Murakami's theory is the idea that an unprecedented and inconceivable event—the atomic bomb blasts in Hiroshima and Nagasaki—might produce in a very specific society an art form that, by virtue of that society's norms and etiquettes, must exist underground. However, it must also, by default, conform to Ezra Pound's classic advice to young artists: "Make it new." By being underground art forms that took years to acquire anything like a mass audience—and that are still acquiring audiences outside of Japan—manga and anime were initially free to develop outside the boundaries of establishment pressures and expectations, and to respond instead more directly to the needs of their readers and viewers.

Not everyone agrees with Murakami, at least not entirely. The San Francisco-based Schodt published his seminal introduction to Japanese comic art, *Manga, Manga*, in 1983, and he became artist Tezuka's official translator in the 1970s. Schodt is one of America's leading authorities on manga and its historical context. "I do think there was a creative exuberance created at the end of the war by the lifting of controls on speech and the fundamental realignment of [Japanese] society," he says. "But if artists had anything political to say, it was more related to a larger political struggle, between progressive leftist forces and those more conservative and traditional. In the '60s and '70s, far more manga artists were reacting to social change and Vietnam than to World War II or the bomb." Still, the idea of an underground art form reacting to deeper societal traumas—as punk rock did in the United Kingdom during the late '70s—may provide a key to unlocking the appeal of Japanese popular culture in America today.

In only its first decade, the twenty-first century has greeted us with trauma galore: a divisive and polemical political structure and an abusive public discourse; seemingly endless war(s) against a faceless, decentralized enemy (with the war on terror, we are fighting an -ism, as they say); radical demographic shifts prompting debates and dilemmas over immigration, language, and religion—the cores of a nation's identity; a hurricane that devastated one our most enduring and idiosyncratic cities; the specter of global climate change and metastasizing viruses; and disintegrating social and manufacturing structures. When you factor in the obvious flip side of technological freedom and fantasy—the freedom of having several selves casts into question the existence of one you can rely upon—you start to believe that fresh ways of narrating the world, new styles of seeing, are not merely plausible, but inevitable.

Of course, it is easy to get seduced by the present. Every age calls itself modern, and so on. Fans and critics of anime who take a historical perspective note the pronounced aesthetic influence of many of Japan's classical traditions—particularly that of *ukiyo-e*, or woodblock prints, and the work of Hokusai, the iconoclastic and prolific artist from Japan's Tokugawa period (eighteenth and nineteenth centuries) who incorporated European influences into his work and revolutionized Japanese art. Hokusai is credited with inventing the term "manga" to identify his smaller, offhand sketches, many of which depict subjects that were considered to be too lowbrow to merit artistic rendering—not unlike the subjects of postwar manga and anime artists in Murakami's underground theory. Manga, according to Schodt, is literally translated as playful, "whimsical pictures," or "pictures made in spite of oneself," as if Hokusai and subsequent artists were helplessly expressing their *honne* truths.

Charles Solomon is a Los Angeles-based animation critic and historian who writes for the *New York Times* and other publications and reviews anime releases on National Public Radio. Solomon's interest in animation began when he was four years old or younger, he says. His extensive knowledge of the history of animation in the United States makes him keenly sensitive to questions of how and why animation from Japan is finding an audience here, not to mention how and why homegrown animation has too often failed to satisfy.

As befits a radio personality, Solomon has a calming, patient voice. He both writes and speaks about anime without alienating his audience with arcane insider references (as so many American otaku seem to do), or insulting them with breathy raves about anime as The Next Big Thing—a posture so often found in anime-focused magazines, print and electronic. The adrenaline rush of Japanophilia hobbles many otherwise knowledgeable discussions of the medium's strengths and weakness.

Solomon is an ideal purveyor of anime style, particularly for those generally older but equally curious Americans who spend fewer waking hours on the Internet. He is convinced that Oscar-winner Miyazaki is "the third genius the art of animation has produced," placing him in the company of Winsor McCay, the creator of *Little Nemo* in the early twentieth century, and Walt Disney.

Solomon's speech gathers speed and volume when I ask him about Murakami's *Little Boy* analysis, which he calls poorly researched. He agrees, however, that traumatic times in the United

States may be connected to the greater embrace of animated, or at least more fantastical, worlds.

"Usually people become more interested in fantasy when the reality around them is not as interesting or satisfying," Solomon says. "The current president's popularity ratings have hit rock bottom. We have this failure in Iraq. And I think the widening gap between rich and poor in this country, the limited opportunities for upward mobility and the loss of manufacturing jobs contribute to this [dissatisfaction]. People are looking for escape and finding it in fantasies." For a parallel, Solomon points to Depression-era America in the 1930s, when, he says, "instead of *Lord of the Rings*, you had Busby Berkeley movies."

But why wouldn't American directors be more than willing and able to provide an animated escape zone, at least as much so as the Japanese?

"In some ways our culture has gotten much more cynical," says Solomon. "That's a problem of a lot of animated films from this country—the characters are so sarcastic and hip, they don't even seem to believe in the story they're in. You don't find that sarcasm in Japanese anime."

Solomon hits on one of the essential features of anime narratives: regardless of how hip, futuristic, high-tech, edgy, and coolly drawn the characters and their surroundings, their essential longings and their interactions with others are presented with a striking degree of sincerity, even when the characters are discussing *mecha* (mechanized/robotic creatures) or biochemical, technologically transmitted viruses.

The Wachowski brothers understood this perfectly in their anime homage, *The Matrix*. Whatever you think of Keanu Reeves's acting, his shell-shocked, nuance-free delivery perfectly suits the sarcasm-free, slightly befuddled search for truth and identity found in so many anime titles.

American novelist David Foster Wallace attacked American irony in the early 1990s, directly so in his essay *E Unibus Pluram: Television and U.S. Fiction*. There he charged American fiction writers with using irony as a defense against a world of overwhelming self-consciousness and media (especially television) saturation, rather than attempting to locate and explore the sincere human spirit and sense of self surviving in its midst. Nearly a decade later, the September 11 attacks produced numerous headlines announcing that irony had reached its limits.

"I think that aspects of anime do appeal to young Americans, specifically at a time when the institutions of government don't seem to represent them," Solomon continues. "They feel powerless. A pervasive theme in a lot of anime is industrial corruption, or military-industrial corruption, that is pervading society and using people against their wills. The vision of shadowy power structures and dark experiments going on does resonate with people today."

anime attacks

About six hours after I landed in Tokyo from New York on the evening of September 11, 2001, Japan time, I watched the black smoke spewing from downtown Manhattan on Japan's national evening news broadcast.

A typhoon had hit Tokyo earlier that day. I arrived at my apartment, slipped off my wet socks, hit the remote. I wanted to know if Tokyo had been damaged by the winds and the rain.

Instead, the evening news carried shots of the north tower of the World Trade Center on a clear day. Japanese television is inordinately focused on American happenings, but I found this weird, especially after a typhoon.

The reporter's voice was shrill, his Japanese fast, barely audible above the thwack of helicopter blades. There followed: Off-kilter shots of planes hitting buildings, some shaky and aerial, some diagonal and shadowy, shot by civilians in the streets below. A crowd of men in suits and ties, women in pant suits and skirts, all with hands covering their mouths, running through the streets wide-eyed, filmed from cameras also in motion. The dust and debris, the eerily beautiful confetti of shredded office paper, computer printouts, receipts, and post-its.

The Pentagon on fire. Planes in the air, locations unverified. Rumors of wreckage in the Midwest. I was on the phone from Japan to America—the line was busy. I was on the Web. Evacuations, bridges and roads closed. Air traffic rerouted. This was really happening.

My neighbors, a Japanese woman and her Irish boyfriend, knocked. They asked if I was okay. I didn't know. Were they?

Finally an email from my mother in Massachusetts arrived. She and all her colleagues were ordered home. My Japanese mother, who had lived with her family in Tokyo's underground shelters more than fifty years earlier while the Americans firebombed and torched the mostly wooden structures above, who had escaped to her father's ancestral home in northern Japan, and was there amid the mountains when the A-bombs fell; the woman who would later marry my father and move to America.

She wrote an email that I printed that night and have since kept laminated in a file: "This is war, Roland. I never thought I'd feel this way again. Not here. Not in America."

In the years since, we have seen many more graphics from 9/11, and have heard some chaotic and sometimes moving audio clips. We have heard from skeptics who present alternate explanations, parallel narratives. We have invaded at least two nations.

But unlike, say, the Zapruder film of the Kennedy assassination, which has become an iconic touchstone of American mystery and tragedy, blurry but singular in its talismanic significance, we do not have a single clear visual image of 9/11. On the one hand, we have amateur and sometimes professional footage shot at angles that are nearly as visually destabilizing and disturbing as the actions they convey. On the other hand, we have magazine covers and wire photos that are almost offensively pristine—too clear, precise, and logical to convey the inconceivability of the event and its aftermath.

Photographs still have their financial drawing power, of course, which is part of what drives photojournalists and paparazzi alike to trek to distant locales or jostle one another to obtain the perfect shot—the magazine or newspaper cover or spread that might one day win an award, and then hang on the wall of a gallery. But it's their mass proliferation, and the proliferation of ways to view and make them, that may have weakened the impact of the photographed event, especially when the event in question defies our conventional narrative logic.

The photographs of torture by American soldiers at Abu Ghraib prison packed a wallop when they appeared, to be sure, particularly the most famous one of the hooded and cloaked prisoner standing atop a cardboard box, his arms outstretched and wired. But these were photos of intimate events, with clearer lines of right and wrong, and a clearer narrative that, however sickening, helped us comprehend and easily ingest their meanings. The photo of the prisoner on the box may have become the most symbolic of the bunch because it seems so mysteriously artful, possessing the rich symbolism of an illustration. The man whose identity is hidden from view is standing in the posture of the crucifix. His conical hood may remind us of Ku Klux Klansmen; the pipes running upward along the wall, the banality of the box, and the crude and twisted wires have echoes of amateur S&M pornography or a fraternity hazing ritual. We can understand the deep and sordid implications of the image before we have been told what it shows, and where it was made.

The reaction to the prison torture photos was significant. But compare it to the fierce reaction months later to the Danish cartoon depicting Mohammed with a bomb in his turban. In the making of the former, human beings were hurt, humiliated, and in some cases killed by the activities they depict. Yet the nature of those activities fits our notions of the banality of evil. In the latter, an artistic reproduction that involved no direct harm in its making created a flashpoint for global tensions, and however unwittingly, a metaphor for misunderstanding.

The London suicide bus bombers and Hurricane Katrina struck within months of each other in the summer of 2005, becoming two of the first major global news stories to be recorded on footage taken by cell phone users, if not the very first. In both cases, cell phone footage was broadcast by professional media outlets attempting to bring viewers closer, attract higher ratings, and make some logical sense of the events themselves.

But how much of that footage is ever rebroadcast? And, more important, how much of it do we remember?

Perhaps there can never be another Zapruder film, or only numerous Zapruder films from a variety of perspectives, each of which is soon forgotten or made irrelevant by the others—which is the same thing.

Steve Alpert is an American who studied art history and Japanese literature. He moved to Japan more than thirty years ago. For the past decade, he has worked for Miyazaki's Studio Ghibli as the Director of International Relations.

I asked him what he loved about anime style.

"The way they used the frame—they weren't afraid to break it!" he said, referring to the volumes of manga he found in Japan in 1974, the year he first visited the country. "You're used to 'wham!' and 'bam!' as an American kid, but what about 'wheeeee' . . . . The perspectives are so evocative. They'll go top down, then from *tatami* (floor) level. Things will get suddenly perverse and violent. These are unbelievable ways of expression. You just don't see that in the cartoon form anywhere else."

Many Americans initially said, often with an air of either numbness or disbelief, what was apparently obvious: 9/11 "looked like a movie." At the time, I'm sure I said something like this as well.

But now I don't think so. I watched carefully throughout that Japanese media-filtered American night, and the odd-angled footage I saw, shot from up, then down, then the running through the streets, scrambling perspective—the absence of cause and effect, the enemies and heroes, the sudden perversity of two massive skyscrapers collapsing in place . . .

What Hollywood director would ask his audience to take seriously the image of the Pentagon on fire, unless in farce? What American artist would narrate evil from the sky, manifest not in missiles from another country, or lasers from a death star empire bent on destroying our quivering cornfields, but in the form of our domestic brand-name airlines?

No one-dimensional superheroes swoop in from the sky; evil seems everywhere; and there is, still today, no mythical happy ending.

The visuals of 9/11 are imprinted on the minds of Americans, young and old, but especially the young—just as the Zapruder film of John F. Kennedy's assassination never left the minds of Americans fifty or older.

But 9/11 doesn't look like a movie, or a photograph. It looks a lot more like anime.

2
atom boys

If manga and anime emerged as underground expressions of trauma in Japan, then their sudden popularity in the United States today means that we are finally hearing another voice in our conversations about atomic bombs, Vietnam, the cultural upheavals of the 1960s and 1970s, and the violence, uncertainties, and fears of the twenty-first century. Japan's popular culture is speaking to us in a visual and psychological language that we may find fresh and entertaining—but it may also be telling us something we need to hear.

James Carroll argues in his book *House of War* that 9/11 was our mushroom cloud, reawakening cold war anxieties over nuclear attack. We have labeled the site of the fallen Twin Towers "ground zero."

We no longer refer to Japan as "the Far East," not only because we fly west to get there, but also because Japan, literally and figuratively, feels a lot closer to us than it used to.

The horrors of Little Boy, the American moniker for the first of the two atomic bombs it detonated in Japan, are easy to find at the Hiroshima Peace Museum. In one memorable display, where you can build your own private narrative of what happened at 8:15 A.M. that August day, charred beans and blackened rice grains in a bento lunch box sit beside the disintegrating uniform of a Japanese schoolboy, its spiky holes blown outward by the radiation, reaching toward you as you peer through the glass.

What is harder to find is any mention of the perpetrator. References to America appear near the very end of the exhibition, mostly in letters written by Hiroshima's mayors to various U.S. presidents, politely but firmly demanding an end to nuclear testing. The exhibit jumps fast from the micro to the macro: Look closely at the results, it seems to be saying. Then: War is hell, and we must prevent it at all costs.

The War Crimes Museum in Ho Chi Minh City stands in striking contrast. Formerly called the American War Crimes Museum (until some Americans suggested losing the reference to gain tourists), the considerably smaller collection is rife with images and artifacts vilifying the aggressors. Photos of U.S. soldiers dragging

Vietnamese bodies tethered to their jeeps; shots of grinning Americans clutching decapitated Vietnamese heads; an internal memo with an official Dow Chemical corporation letterhead noting that the war presented near-perfect conditions for testing the efficacy of Agent Orange, the cancerous herbicide and defoliant sprayed by U.S. planes over Vietnam for at least a decade.

These are radically different wars and conditions, to be sure. And Japan's guilt over its own decisive, aggressive role in World War II is no doubt part of the reason behind its reluctance to point fingers, as is the nation's critical political, economic, and military alliance with its former conquerors today.

But it is also true that in the wake of the two atomic bombs—the most immediately destructive weapons used in human history thus far—not to mention the firebombing of its cities (which ultimately killed many more than the A-bombs did), Japan avidly embraced the products of American popular culture.

Shortly after the war, it was almost impossible not to.

"American culture was overwhelming!" says the novelist Haruki Murakami, speaking to me during one of his periodic residencies in the United States, where his books are critically acclaimed and commercially successful. Murakami is a baby boomer, born just after the war in Kyoto. His fiction incorporates numerous American influences—literary, cultural, and commercial—and he spends a good deal of his time translating iconic American authors, such as F. Scott Fitzgerald and Raymond Carver, into Japanese.

"When I was in my teens in the sixties," Murakami recalls, "America was so big. Everything was shiny and bright. When I was fifteen years old, I went to see Art Blakey and the Jazz Messengers in Kobe. I was so impressed. Those were very good days for American culture."

Murakami also suggests that the image of America was more complex in the postwar years, and that our so-called culture wars of the '60s and early '70s were actually a part of our international appeal. "America had two sides: the strong side, and the youthful, countercultural side. We [Japanese] criticized the Vietnam War, but we were still listening to Jimi Hendrix and the Doors."

Murakami's friend and fellow boomer, Motoyuki Shibata, is a scholar of American literature at the University of Tokyo and Japan's leading translator of contemporary American literature. Their generation of postwar Japanese, he says, looked to America as a model of what they might become, and as a motivator for self-transformation. "America was one place we were hopefully headed for. We had respect for American democracy and individualism, although we didn't know those words yet."

The abstraction of blame at the museum in Hiroshima may also have something to do with the nature of the technology that produced the trauma. It is not hard to imagine your rage at an attacker holding you at gunpoint in a back alley, or a soldier thrusting a bayonet toward you, or troops landing on your shores and firing machine guns from trenches. These are more intimate and more immediately logical transgressions against you. And they have faces, nationalities.

But an event that decimates entire cities and their populations in a single instant—that is harder to get your head around. The Japanese word for the bomb, coined literally before they knew what had hit them, expresses the deeper bewilderment. What we called Little Boy the Japanese called *pika-don*, an onomatopoeic term. *Pika* is a sudden extremely bright light, such as lightning, and *don* is a thunderous blast, like fireworks exploding, or something very heavy falling to the floor. It is the same *pika* that appears in Pikachu—the Pokemon with the power to unleash lightning bolts from his tail. *Chu* is Japanese onomatopoeia for the sound of a mouse.

9/11 may have, for the first time, imbued Americans with a similar sense of bewilderment. And by stating this I am not equating the horrors of that American day with the instant devastation of two atomic bombs. But the lasting aura of 9/11 may be similar: immediate transformation, a sudden shift in a mass population from the known risks and vulnerabilities to the unknown, the abstract, the shadowy, and the faceless—and the imminent possibility of an apocalyptic event on a sunny bright morning.

Philip Roth once wrote that it was no longer possible for the contemporary novelist to compete with the daily stories in newspaper headlines. That did not stop Roth from becoming one of America's most prolific novelists, but it did raise crucial questions about the capacity of a medium, the novel in his case, to coexist successfully with the rapidly evolving environment in which its readers have to live.

For reasons both aesthetic and cultural, anime seems to be a medium ideally poised to explore our contemporary sensibilities. And it does not seem accidental that some of the most popular titles in contemporary America, *Akira*, *Ghost in the Shell*, and *Evangelion*, portray worlds in which sudden transformations in shadowy environs (where daylight is extinguished in an instant, where playful schoolyard boys and girls become warriors, and where everyone is either wedded to or partly composed of the machinations of technology) have apocalyptic and unreliable narrative threads sewn into the fabric of their mise-en-scène.

In some respects, anime's relationship to verisimilitude, to what we expect and demand from portrayals of reality, is freer than that of most other forms of visual expression. As the American anime scholar and author Susan Napier points out, this is one of the challenges that some viewers—particularly older viewers who may have always considered any form of animation kid's fare—confront when they attempt to enter sophisticated, adult-oriented narratives via the anime medium.

"We're less defended when we get into anime," says Napier, citing a psychologist's explanation for the medium's destabilizing effects on neophyte viewers. "We have certain expectations from the film world, but anime can do what it damn well pleases. It goes way down into our deep [psychological] structures, and that can be really scary."

That can also be, for those viewers assaulted by visual media clichés and manipulations who seek a deeper engagement with their art forms, underground or not, really thrilling.

osamu tezuka

The summer of the atom bombs, Osamu Tezuka was a seventeen-year-old boy in Osaka.

Often called Japan's second city, Osaka and its residents firmly distinguish themselves from their Tokyo brethren. Osaka produces the majority of the nation's entertainers, in comedy, music, and film. It is considered funkier, friendlier, and cruder than Tokyo, which must bear the weight of Japan's major institutions: its national government, financial center, bastions of high culture, and mass media. If New York, Los Angeles, and Washington, D.C., were mashed into one cramped and overpopulated metropolis, you might approximate Tokyo in the United States. If the sensibility of Chicago's South Side and the eccentricities of pre-Katrina New Orleans could be crammed into one town, you might approximate Osaka's place in the Japanese cityscape.

Tezuka was raised in relative wealth; his family was cultured and upper middle class, and as a child in the mid-'30s he was able to view 8-millimeter prints of Disney and other American and European films in his own home. As with so many Japanese boys (including Miyazaki and Satoshi Tajiri, creator of Pokemon), especially those who become artists, Tezuka's hobby was collecting insects. In fact, much of Japanese anime design emanates from this insect obsession. Think of Ultraman's praying-mantis eyes, the beetlelike space ships in *Battle of the Planets*, and just about any Japanese sci-fi robot or monster, which often feature enlarged insect appendages that appear to have been magnified—or irradiated.

Tezuka studied to be a doctor, but he preferred drawing, and in the aftermath of the war he took advantage of two key shifts in Japan. As Schodt and others point out, the near collapse of the Japanese publishing industry at the end of the war opened up the field to risk-taking independent presses, which were largely responsible for distributing the new medium. And the lifting of long-standing censorship laws enabled Tezuka and his ilk to blast the lid off a Pandora's box of creative expression.

Manga, and later anime, was cheap to make, relatively easy to distribute, and virtually free of intrusive meddling, editorial or otherwise.

Tezuka is where today's anime style starts, though many Americans remain unfamiliar with his name and his works. He was the beginning of what is referred to today by the *Super #1 Robot* author and lifelong anime fan Matt Alt as "the Mobius strip" of interrelations between Japanese and American artists—a cross-pollination of influences that traverses the realms of computer-generated images (CGI), limited or two-dimensional animation, and live action.

I am hunched over on a low leather sofa in the brightly lit meeting room of Tezuka Productions, one of two studios that continue to operate after Tezuka's death in 1989. The studio is located in Takadanobaba, Tokyo, near the campus of Waseda University. In the original story, the Mighty Atom / Astro Boy was created by a scientist at Waseda as a replacement for his deceased son—in the then futuristic year, 2003.

Framed portraits of the artist's most famous characters—Atom/Astro, Kimba the White Lion, BlackJack—line the walls, eyeing me like family members from a faraway land.

Yoshihiro Shimizu, who worked alongside Tezuka for eleven years, is flipping through various panels of the artist's work. Shimizu, a lean, smartly dressed man in his late fifties, is focused, intent upon showing me the range and depth of his former boss's manga.

"The U.S. influenced him dramatically," Shimizu says, singling out the works of Disney and Max Fleischer, the Austrian-born animation pioneer responsible for bringing *Betty Boop* and *Superman* to the movie screen, among other achievements. "Also, he loved movies in general. And he loved the natural world." He loved *Bambi* so much that he claimed to have seen it eighty times, memorizing the film from start to finish.

In Tezuka's print work, you can see the "broken frame" that drew Alpert into the kinetic Japanese style—the sheer unpredictable movement of the visuals. Shimizu explains that Tezuka was frustrated by earlier comic renderings, which bore a greater resemblance to the staging of a play: one character enters stage left, exits stage right, and so on. He wanted to apply the freer movements of cinema to the comic format.

Tezuka's early work looks strikingly contemporary, almost hauntingly so. Shimizu shows me his use of the sudden close-up panel amid an action scene, the "panning" panels across peripheral settings, the diverse "camera" shots of a single scene, and the hero whose raised fist does indeed plunge past the borders of the frame.

But he also reveals to me Tezuka's apparent fearlessness. Aside from the American influences cited earlier (visible in the wide eyes and rounder shapes of Tezuka's work versus that of others in the anime tradition), the artist was also deeply drawn to the natural world, to the organic and fecund. There is an earthiness to Tezuka's subject matter, a willingness to confront, for example, the messiness of the human body (characters vomit, spew mucus, fornicate with sounds and sensations, and so on), the spectral lushness of a natural landscape, or the intimate physicality of violence.

One scene shows a Nazi kicking a Jewish woman; in another, a full page is devoted to a samurai warrior who, after committing ritual suicide, is discovered by his lover, his body bent double, his head resting in a pool of blood and innards. Raskolnikov is shown in graphic detail ax-murdering his elderly female landlord in panels of *Crime and Punishment*. A final panel shows a massive field of human figures, their bodies melting in the wake of a blast.

Dark stuff for any medium, let alone comics.

Tezuka created the blueprint for Japanese manga and anime artists—and it was vast. All subject matter was fair game, and expressions could be bleak, violent, and apocalyptic, in addition to being humorous and hopeful. His major works included multivolume projects such as *Buddha*, which retells the story of Siddhartha in often graphically violent and erotic detail, and *Phoenix*, about the mythical bird who, in Tezuka's rendering, appears in the distant future, and whose blood can render humans immortal.

"He focused on story, and he was a voracious reader of both eastern and western sources," explains Shimizu. "When we shifted from manga to anime, his focus on story was critical. We didn't have enough money to compete with the American studios. So our character's mouths don't move as much, and the backgrounds don't change as often. But the stories are really good. The depth of character, the variety of subject matter. And we don't need to have happy endings."

Tezuka's first major comic book, *Mighty Atom*, appeared in magazine serial form in 1952 and on Japanese TV sets in 1963. According to Shimizu, the U.S. title was changed to *Astro Boy* because the son of an NBC executive said that "mighty atom" somehow reminded him of a fart. A more plausible explanation: DC comics' series from the 1940s, *The Atom*, was frequently referred to as "The Mighty Atom," and NBC's lawyers were keen to avoid a copyright battle with the comics giant.

Whatever the real reason, the title change helped put Tezuka's creation on American TV screens in 1964, when a portion of the 193 original episodes aired in translation in New York. The schizophrenic "Astro/Atom" title has since caused Tezuka's Japanese studio numerous copyright-related headaches. In another twist of the Mobius strip, both titles have been incorporated into the Japanese edition: its title on Japanese TV is *Astro Robot Mighty Atom*.

Tezuka met his hero, Walt Disney, at the 1964 World's Fair in New York. The American allegedly told Tezuka that he admired *Astro Boy* and wanted to create something like it. A framed photograph of the two shaking hands still hangs in the entranceway of the Tezuka home.

The smiling public face of Tezuka and Disney's relationship is typical of Japanese *tatemae*, and in this instance, the mutual admiration between the two artists is well documented. But it belies a few less savory events in the careers of the two studios.

A strong rumor persists that the Disney company's *The Lion King*, released in 1994, five years after Tezuka's death, plagiarized numerous story and character elements from Tezuka's *Kimba the White Lion*, released thirty years earlier. The rumor is stoked frequently by anime fans on both sides of the Pacific, on Web sites offering detailed analyses of the parallels (which are difficult to ignore, starting with the main character's name, which is Simba in the Disney film) and in several books. The rumor has been featured in an episode of *The Simpsons*. Was Tezuka's studio paid hush money by Disney, as some have confidently alleged?

"Zero," Shimizu replies, making an "O" with his fingers. After reflecting on Tezuka's admiration of Disney, he offers the company's official line. "We think it's a totally different story. Kimba is part human, part animal. The lion king is just an animal. Of course, we were urged to sue Disney by some in our industry. But we're a small, weak company. It wouldn't be worth it anyway. We received letters from lawyers in places like Iowa and Hawaii, offering to take up the case." He laughs. "Disney's lawyers are among the top twenty in the world!"

Still smiling, he excuses himself, and then returns with two handsome hardbacks featuring *Bambi* and *Snow White*. He leafs through them, showing me some of the pages. The illustrations are definitely Disney-like, but something about the lines is a bit off—a little shakier, perhaps, less assured, but also more complex.

Tezuka loved the Disney stories and illustrations so much, he copied them line for line—not from comic books, but by going to the movie theater and sitting with his sketch pad through several showings of the Disney films. The books he produced were originally sold on the streets of Japan in the 1950s, without Disney's knowledge or permission. The copies Shimizu is showing me are reprints, issued a few years ago as collector's items. Disney now collects 50 percent of the sales.

Shimizu's implication is clear: the relationship between the two artists is what counts—not the legal issues, not the profits (though it would be interesting to compare the balance sheets for Tezuka's print homage with those of Disney's megahit movie and musical). "If Tezuka were alive when *Lion King* was released," he concludes, "and if he knew about even the rumor that Disney might have copied elements of his work, he would have been proud."

The careers of both artists provide fodder for understanding not only their aesthetics, but also their homelands, the characteristics that define both nations. Walt Disney liked to say that his most famous creation, Mickey Mouse, embodied distinctly American virtues—he is charming, friendly, open, and industrious, always there when you need him.

So I ask Shimizu: What makes Astro Boy especially Japanese?

His answer is surprisingly decisive: "He's troubled. And he worries. A lot."

Shimizu continues to address the gray areas that characterize Japanese anime in general—the absence of easily definable dilemmas, moralities, or resolutions that run through the form to the current day, from *Gundam* to *Ghost in the Shell*. Japan is a nation without a morally prescriptive central religion; neither the native form of Buddhism nor the national faith, Shinto, proffer commandments for moral behavior, or a holy book by which to live your life. A greater emphasis is placed on contexts, how to behave in a given situation when confronted by a specific set of circumstances.

In a globalizing world that has grown less centralized and less certain by the year, Japan's comparatively case-by-case approach to life's innumerable narratives could be remarkably, if coincidentally, well suited to the age.

Japan is an island situated between the United States and China, Shimizu reasons, taking us straight into contemporary geopolitics. "We understand both sides, and we have to base our decisions considering those two sides. It's the dilemma of being between two worlds, two hemispheres, and understanding, even sympathizing with both. Disney is always pushing the good side, the morally right. But the in-between world speaks to the Japanese."

Shimizu's is the most compelling explanation I have yet heard about the overwhelming prevalence of dualistic and transforming characters in anime and manga. These range from Tezuka's half-robot Astro Boy and half-human Kimba the Lion, to the androgynous or transforming gender of some of his robot characters (seen especially in today's female-targeted *shojo* stories), to the half-mechanized men and women doing battle in the more apocalyptic films of the past twenty years. And the relative aesthetic freedom of animation versus live action (with its recognizable actors and relative verisimilitude) can make such dualism believable.

Tezuka's numerous achievements (he is called the god of anime by some) are too many to mention here, and they are addressed in several books that cover his life and career. But the conflict that can result from "being between two worlds" has a curious place within the industry he helped to create.

Tezuka's embrace of the television medium, from the 1960s onward, also turned out to be a trap—not merely for himself, but for generations of anime artists. What is referred to somewhat discreetly by industry insiders as "the curse of Osamu" goes something like this: In the early '60s, when Japanese television first began broadcasting anime series, Tezuka was the leading artist. Producers naturally sought his work, and Tezuka set the price at an absurdly low (roughly) $3,000 per episode—which would have been significantly less in real value forty-odd years ago.

The result was, and is, that no one could ask for a higher price. Tezuka, already from a privileged background and having established himself as the leading manga and anime artist of his era, was able to forge ahead, dominating the Japanese airwaves with his titles while competing studios dropped out of sight. Essentially, Tezuka was dumping, selling his episodes for cheap to keep others out.

"Many of the older anime producers are screwed, even today," says David d'Heilly, founder of 2dk, an art, design, and event production company with offices in Tokyo and New York. "And Tezuka screwed them."

There are milder opinions and attempts to justify Tezuka's decisions. He desperately wanted his art form to "spread throughout Japan," says Shizu Yuasa, d'Heilly's wife and partner at 2dk. Sitting in their airy apartment and head office in West Tokyo, Yuasa is quick to defend Tezuka's intentions. "It worked! It's one of the reasons we have so much rich animation in Japan. He didn't want to compete with other anime producers; he wanted to be able to compete with foreign programs and other types of programs on the market."

D'Heilly is not so sure. "There were other ways he could have done that. In 1964, he basically looked at other animators and said, 'I'll see you, and I'll *lower* you.' It's the irony of the curse that the master of anime, the father of the form, strangled so many of his children."

This 2dk debate is emblematic of the mixed regard for Tezuka inside the anime industry. His decision to set the price so low meant that the sponsors—giant advertising firms like Dentsu—control all the rights to anime titles broadcast on TV, limiting both the aesthetic and financial parameters of the medium.

Tezuka's own original studio, Mushi Productions, is where *Astro Boy* was actually created by the artist more than fifty years ago. Literally and figuratively, it is nowhere near the Takadanobaba headquarters of Tezuka Productions.

Mushi Productions is housed in a rundown warehouse on a narrow and nondescript suburban side street. Its interior is cramped and poorly lit; an old VCR teeters atop a shelf piled high with papers and magazines, its cord leading to several dusty multiple-outlet adaptors, each crammed with plugs.

Mushi went bankrupt in 1973 but was revived four years later, after negotiations with several television networks. Tezuka appointed Satoshi Ito, a staff member, to oversee studio operations, a position Ito maintains today. But there were fewer and fewer operations, and, as Ito points out, "Tezuka supervised the first anime titles we made [in the late '70s], but it was no longer his company."

The loss of financial and artistic control is an unavoidable part of Tezuka's legacy, complicating his reputation in Japan and frustrating (or infuriating) later generations of anime artists—notably one who would begin to assume the mantle of anime master while Tezuka was still alive: Hayao Miyazaki.

hayao miyazaki

Miyazaki is anime's best-known figurehead in the United States—an Oscar-winning director whose films, especially on home video and DVD, have become standards for many Americans with children. In Japan, he is beloved. He and his Studio Ghibli are also, artistically and financially, the envy of the anime industry.

Animators in Japan typically make far less money off a hit production than do Hollywood screenwriters—or even the original
authors of the manga on which the productions are usually
based. Miyazaki is the exception. *Spirited Away* is the highest-
grossing film in Japanese cinema history; the third highest is his
1999 release, *Princess Mononoke*.

But Miyazaki's success and the global reach of his work are
exceptional in other ways. He has not pursued the overseas merchandising model that has made other Japanese cultural products, such as Pokemon, Hello Kitty, and Yu-Gi-Oh, mass-produced
stateside sensations. He generally shuns interviews, and while he
will make appearances in Europe and the United States at major
festivals or upon the release of his films, it is hard to imagine him
taking up residence in either place the way that both novelist
Haruki Murakami and artist Takashi Murakami have (they are not
related).

Twenty years ago, Eiko Tanaka produced two of Miyazaki's
films, *My Neighbor Totoro* and *Kiki's Delivery Service*, both enormously popular with American kids and their parents. She
later left Ghibli to found her own studio, and she sees Miyazaki
and Ghibli as a model for the entire industry. "Five years from
now, we [Studio4C] would like to have accomplished as much as
Miyazaki and Ghibli have, and reach the rest of the world as he
does. That's the reason I founded this company. Success in
America is our goal."

Other animators, in Japan and elsewhere, revere Miyazaki's
artistry. Illustrated, framed, and sometimes breathless tributes
("You're our inspiration, Miyazaki-san!") hang along the stairwell
of Studio Ghibli's headquarters, one signed by the artists at U.S.
animation giant Pixar (including John Lasseter, one of America's
top animators and now a friend of Miyazaki's), another by Nick
Park and his staff at Aardman Studios of the U.K., creators of
Wallace and Gromit and *Chicken Run*. Park has also visited Tokyo
and befriended Miyazaki, and many Ghibli staff artists are big fans
of *Wallace and Gromit*. Anime artists in Japan often cite Miyazaki's
first two feature films, *The Castle of Cagliostro* and *Nausicaa of the
Valley of the Wind*, as masterpieces of the form.

Tezuka was an inspiration for the young Miyazaki, who painstakingly copied the older artist's manga just as Tezuka did Disney's drawings. At some point, however, perhaps sensing the anxiety of influence, Miyazaki realized he needed to develop his own style—and by some accounts, burned his Tezuka imitations.

His differences with Tezuka ran deeper than the television dumping curse, though that was clearly a part of it. Miyazaki deeply resented television as a medium for his work. Ghibli's Alpert says that in addition to the dire financial conditions, "he felt the medium was just too limiting. He would say: 'Why does the story have to be 27 minutes long?' "

"Basically, Miyazaki couldn't have enough control over production with TV," adds Tezuka's Shimizu. "You were always bowing to the sponsors."

While Miyazaki admired Tezuka's manga, he found Tezuka's television animations to be lowbrow, even crude—and not just because of the medium. Shimizu tells of a published critique that Miyazaki wrote of an earlier independent film made by Tezuka in 1962 named *Story of a Certain Street Corner*, a short anime containing a scene where a poster violently burns in the midst of war.

"Miyazaki wrote that the scene was just too sad, too depressing," Shimizu says. "And he went on to say that Tezuka took the themes of death and loss far too lightly. Tezuka was not fully respected by Miyazaki."

In the last decade of his life, Tezuka stopped making series for TV, willing to produce only two-hour specials or features for the medium instead. And he was alive to see the box office successes of Miyazaki's first two feature films, *Castle* and *Nausicaa*, which earned hundreds of thousands of dollars. "He was aware of that," notes Shimizu. "Everyone was."

By taking anime straight to the cinema—which was one of Tezuka's primary inspirations for expanding the form—Miyazaki had escaped the curse of Osamu.

Miyazaki, too, was born into money. His family owned Miyazaki Airplane, a company that made rudders for the Japanese air force's Zero fighter planes. His father was the managing director.

Some critics suggest that Miyazaki has always felt guilt over his family's profiting from the war, and that his later political stances—he was a Marxist and a labor leader—were partly shaped by a deeply felt antielitism. He headed the labor union in his first job at Toei Animation, and it's easy to detect his disdain for adult pretensions in his work. His protagonists are children, people who haven't learned to discriminate between economic classes. And his films repeatedly feature the children in glamorous images of flight, loosed from the pedestrian concerns of the adults below.

"Miyazaki's main characters look to be about ten at the beginnings of his films," says Tanaka. "By the end, they have the heart and mind of a sixteen-year-old. They grow and mature dramatically through his stories."

Most poignant in his films is a sense of loss—a quality of melancholy for a more natural and more richly fantastical world—combined with a sense of possibility, a hope for recovery. As scholar Napier writes in *Anime from Akira to Howl's Moving Castle*: "[Miyazaki's] vision is not only of 'what is lost' . . . but also, perhaps most importantly, what could be." She describes Miyazaki's renderings of both a prewar innocence and natural beauty and also a postwar, apocalyptic barrenness.

Because Miyazaki is unabashed about producing films for children, his anime aesthetic may be more attuned to American expectations of the animated form. But because he explores complex layers of longing, possibility, pathos, and redemption, his films also draw in the adults (whether parents or childless fans) who appreciate the sophistication, and ambition, of his stories, not to mention the sheer beauty of his visuals.

Studio Ghibli is located some distance from central Tokyo, in the city's far western suburbs, where so many other anime producers set up shop twenty to thirty years ago, on what was then relatively cheap land. With Ghibli, though, you get the feeling that Miyazaki himself might prefer the distance, whatever the cost. His chosen "bed town," as suburban neighborhoods were once called in Japan, is quiet and well maintained, with notably more trees and vegetation than is normally found in Tokyo's sprawl. A stroll to the studio passes a plot of wide-open land (a rarity anywhere in urban Japan), a playground rife with chattering kindergarten children bearing bright yellow hats, and a horticultural nursery, all evoking scenes from Miyazaki's films.

The studio complex consists of three buildings, the newest of which was constructed after the success of *Spirited Away*. With an interior of polished wood and high-peaked cathedral ceilings, the house has the openness and airiness of a modern house in the forest, perhaps somewhere in the Pacific Northwest. It seems stylishly rural.

In the main building, which is more utilitarian, though roomy for Tokyo, Alpert guides me through a variety of interconnected rooms. In one, a team of in-betweeners—apprentice artists, most of whom are in their twenties to early thirties and who sketch in the subtle movements characters make between key frames or shots—hover in intense concentration over tidy, fluorescent-lit desks. It's unglamorous, solitary work, and it is how Miyazaki himself got his start at giant Toei Animation in the early 1960s.

In producer and longtime friend Toshio Suzuki's office on the top floor, Miyazaki's 2003 Oscar statuette sits in a case of collectibles, including a samurai sword and his Golden Bear from the 2002 Berlin Film Festival.

On the ground floor, Alpert shows me still images taken directly from Miyazaki's films. The artist's obsession with flight is exemplified in many of the stills, including one from 1992's *Porco Rosso*, which is about an Italian World War I fighting ace. The still shows Fio, the young female flight engineer, soaring high above sea and land, seen from slightly above and to the side. "The perspective in that still," Alpert says. "No one else could have drawn that." Standing before another nearby still from 1989's *Kiki's Delivery Service*, this one also showing a young girl in flight, Alpert urges me to focus on Kiki's hair blowing in the wind. "Look at the details in that shot. Miyazaki works so hard."

Alpert first arrived in Japan over thirty years ago, having studied Japanese literature at Columbia University under noted American scholars and translators Donald Keene and

Edward Seidensticker. An art history major in college, and a long-time Japanese film buff, he was attracted not only to the look of manga, but also to its myriad contents.

"I couldn't believe the inventiveness of the subject matter—about everything. From monsters and sex and baseball and housewives, to instructions on the Japanese economy."

Though manga sales have slowed domestically, that the inventiveness remains amid the plethora of visual distractions now available is a testament to the enduring nature of the form in Japan. Mountainous racks of manga, published weekly, greet visitors at magazine shops, bookstores, manga cafés, and train station kiosks, organized across a full spectrum of titles, series, and contents. It is difficult to imagine a topic not covered in cartoon form in Japan.

Before joining Ghibli ten years ago, Alpert worked for Disney in their Tokyo office. Ghibli could hardly have picked a more suitable employee for their international department. Alpert had also worked for Citibank; he knew how to deal with the fine print, he knew how Disney worked, and he is fluently bilingual.

He fast became a Miyazaki fan, one who served as a critical bridge between the two companies and cultures, establishing the contract for Disney's distribution of Miyazaki's films in the United States.

"I was still at Disney," he recalls, "and for some odd reason, no one had ever purchased Ghibli rights in the United States. So in order to convince the executives, we went straight to the animators in the U.S."

Alpert took his passion further. To entice Disney executives, he made a documentary film of American animators raving over Miyazaki's genius, boasting of their bootlegs of Miyazaki films in Japanese, and showing off the little Totoro figurines on their desks and the Ghibli books in their drawers. He even made a soundtrack.

"Executives have short attention spans," he explains. "We basically prepared the Disney executives for what they should buy, making sure they understood the value. We had to get to Eisner through them."

The strategy was successful. In 1996, Studio Ghibli entered into a distribution deal with Disney that would ensure that Americans would have access to Miyazaki's magic. At the cinema, where Miyazaki naturally prefers that his work be seen, we were treated to translated prints of *Princess Mononoke*, *Spirited Away*, and *Howl's Moving Castle*. At home, all of Miyazaki's major titles became available, in English, on videocassette.

But the deal had a hitch, and it has worked entirely in Ghibli's favor. Yasuyoshi Tokuma, the producer who financed the founding of Ghibli, and who died four years after signing the Disney deal as the parent company of Ghibli, opted to keep all digital rights.

"And Disney wasn't fuming," says Alpert, leaning toward me with a stunned and wide-eyed expression. "They were the last studio to catch on to the value of digital rights. And part of it was Michael Eisner's greed. He was like: 'We're the most popular video rights holder in the universe, so they won't have a new technology if we don't participate.' " Alpert leans back in his chair, his head shaking slowly from side to side. "Guess again, Michael. Guess again . . ."

Stories of Japanese anime, game, and toy producers signing away millions of dollars to their American distributors are almost an industry cliché. Partly because Japan is a less contract-based, less litigious, and less openly assertive society, and partly because many companies fail to comprehend the value of intellectual property rights, Japanese executives frequently accept lump sums that at first seem generous, then rapidly pale in comparison with percentages of sales. To some, it is delicious irony to have turned the tables on Disney.

While it is not clear that Tokuma knew that the DVD would become as ubiquitous as the compact disk, it is certain that Ghibli is a notable, and profitable, Japanese exception. The other notable one is Sanrio, which has kept their paws tightly wrapped around Hello Kitty.

Despite *Spirited Away*'s Academy Award, *My Neighbor Totoro* is probably Miyazaki's signature film in the United States. The story is of a family in rural Japan struggling with illness. The film's portrayal of the two sisters, a stern but loving father, and the eponymous furry forest creature who provides solace, comfort, and practical help when the girls need to visit their dying mother, has become a symbol of anime's strengths in America—especially for families.

But what exactly is Totoro? Like Pikachu and its legions, Totoro has no direct model in the biological world. *Totoro* was originally made in conjunction with another consecrated anime classic, *Grave of the Fireflies*, directed by Ghibli's other in-house master, Isao Takahata. The pairing of the two had partly to do with theatrical demands: Japanese cinemas at the time (the late '80s) refused to run a single anime film in one showing. Since *Grave* was based on an autobiographical book by Akiyuki Nosaka, whose sister died during the war from malnutrition, it was considered the safer bet.

But it was also an aesthetic pairing, a kind of collaboration on separate projects. Both directors chose the same starting point: their childhood experiences during the war. Takahata, who is six years' Miyazaki's senior, set the beginning of his story in Tokyo, focusing on the trials of those who were still in the city during the United States military's firebombing campaigns. A haunting scene of the homeless and the dying opens the film. *Grave*'s protagonist children, a brother and his younger sister, are sent into the countryside for safety—the very fate of many Japanese, including Miyazaki.

In *Grave*, the countryside rapidly turns dark. The desperation and selfishness of the other characters, which may be necessary for their own survival, and the pride and love of the older brother gradually force the siblings to go it alone.

Miyazaki skips the city and the war's immediate presence entirely, beginning with the children's arrival in an exquisitely beautiful rural setting. But the war is a powerful subtext in the film, and Miyazaki's subtle references to it are most vivid to those who experienced it. The little boy, Kanta, is seen wearing adult's clothing vaguely resembling a uniform that has been reconfigured (and restitched) and that barely fits him. The automobiles are drawn in detail to match the styles and makes available to rural residents during a time of scarcity.

"Older Japanese people from the countryside immediately identify these signs," says Alpert. "And even older urban Japanese who lived in rural Japan immediately see the war in *Totoro*."

Both films are remarkable testaments to a generation's experience of trauma conveyed through a medium of powerful expression. *Grave* is particularly powerful. Sibling love, particularly between brother and sister, is rarely conveyed well in any medium. And *Grave*'s central conflict is as heartwrenching as it is complex; the older brother's determination, self-reliance, pride, and sense of devotion to his sister—so often seen as heroic and honorable characteristics in children's narratives—is what drives him to make a decision that ultimately puts their lives in jeopardy.

What marks Miyazaki's vision, aside from the sunnier disposition of the characters the children meet, is the sense of mystery and magic in the natural world. As Napier eloquently describes: "*Totoro* effectively create[s] a low-key sense of the enchantment lurking in daily life." This is a far cry from the genial chirpiness or wisecracking sassiness of so many of Disney's animated animals, especially the recent ones, who often seem perpetually pumped up by antidepressants, or else infallibly wise.

Some of Miyazaki's low-key enchantment emanates from a technical decision: he uses silence. As critic Charles Solomon has written in the *New York Times*, recent American animations have grown increasingly garrulous, with characters spewing out dialogue at a rapid-fire pace, addling the audience with a constant stream of asides and jokes. But that has not always been the case.

"Since MTV and the increasing battle for audience attention spans in this country, fewer American filmmakers are willing to risk losing the audience," he tells me via telephone from L.A. "If you look back at the great animated films in this country, though, you see that *Bambi*, for example, has about 1,000 words in the entire film."

Silence and stillness are legendary features of Japan's traditional arts. In Noh theater, as Solomon points out, it may take an entire play for an actor to make it across the stage. Zen Buddhism emphasizes silence and stillness in meditation to a radical degree, and Japanese gardens are notable for their restraint and solemnity. Japanese rock gardens, of course, do not move at all, at least not visibly.

But there are many counterexamples in the culture, especially on Japan's hyperkinetic urban thoroughfares, where the constant coursing of crowds traversing streets and escalators and riding in glass-walled elevators is complemented by relentlessly streaming neon advertisements, five-story video screens, and elevated trains rattling above. Prerecorded and live voices welcome you into storefronts, advise you to be careful, and thank you for stopping by.

The question of context, of each situation demanding a different approach, is relevant here. After hours (or when the trains shut down), Tokyo and other Japanese cities can become very quiet. A standard, bleating irritation of the New York night, the car alarm, is all but absent from Tokyo. And because of the circuitous layout of Tokyo's streets, many residences are tucked behind or away from the sounds of nocturnal activities. In Manhattan during the summer, an open window can invite all sorts of sleep-depriving sounds, from the rumble of garbage trucks to boomboxes to inebriated club or bar crawlers gabbing at high volume as they smoke cigarettes on the sidewalk. But while Tokyo has at least as many all-night venues as New York, their sounds seem to remain venue-bound.

Of course there are exceptions. When my sister visited recently and opened the window of her hotel room for fresh air, she found the noise of Shinjuku, a major neighborhood, intolerable.

Anime artists like Miyazaki and Takahata may be able to trust their anime audiences more because the form, dating back to Tezuka's series in the early '60s, is not so alien to the Japanese, and their expectations for a sophisticated experience are higher. Pixar's Lasseter also points to *Totoro* as an example of anime's effective use of quiet. "So few words of dialogue in so many minutes of film," says Solomon. "And the results are much more satisfying than some of the stuff here in America, which looks like it was edited in a Cuisinart."

Nostalgia is often a mask for rage. The intensity with which we yearn for a lost world is frequently proportionate to the discomfort we feel in our own. Think of the violence in the Hollywood western genre—most popular when American society was redefining itself in the '50s and '60s, healing postwar traumas with reassurances of freedom and sometimes brutal justice.

It is impossible not to sense the anger in Miyazaki's *Spirited Away*, however exquisite its tableaux.

I first saw *Spirited Away* in a theater in New York. The excitement expressed by friends who had already seen it in Japan made me particularly sensitive to what I watched on the screen. The most memorable image of the film for me was the sudden transformation of ten-year-old girl Chihiro's parents into monstrous pigs.

The scene occurs early on, after the father takes a wrong turn and the family gets lost, finding themselves at the entrance to a dark tunnel.

On the other side is an abandoned amusement park. Chihiro's father suggests that it may have been built during the peak of Japan's bubble economy of the '80s.

Suddenly, the parents are overwhelmed by the smell of apparently irresistible cooking from a nearby food stall, whose visual motifs imply that it serves Chinese eats.

When Chihiro is less than enthusiastic, the father tells her not to worry. He has a credit card.

As they dig into the food, the parents lose control of their appetites—and the proportions of their physical selves. They become pigs, enormous and violent in their loss of self-control. Previously well-dressed, upper-middle-class urban professionals driving an Audi, the mother and father turn into helpless gluttons, their faces swollen and squint-eyed as they overstuff them, their fleshy waists drooping over their belt loops.

Only after Chihiro, appalled by the sight, leaves her pig parents to their grunting and snuffling does she gain access to another of Miyazaki's enchanted realms.

Miyazaki's harsh portrait of the parents—a generation that came of age when the austerity of Japan's postwar years had long receded—strikes me as an exceptional condemnation, jolted to life by artistic adrenaline. It's the kind of impulsive burst of violent emotion (or just violence or just emotion) that I associate with America's auteur-driven films of the '60s and '70s, from a Kubrick, Coppola, or Scorsese. Like those films, *Spirited Away* was released without being vetted by a focus group to question whether such a scene belongs in an animated film for children.

The freedom Japan's anime directors enjoy is not merely the by-product of a society that codifies public and private selves, making space for after-hours fantasies. From Tezuka to Miyazaki, to far less proven talents, for good or for ill, this idea is built into the industry itself.

One of Tanaka's directors at Studio4C is an American named Michael Arias. Arias was raised in the United States "on both coasts," he says, attended Wesleyan for a year, then graduated from NYU. After creating special effects for Hollywood films (*Total Recall*, among others), he moved to Japan fifteen years ago. He rarely goes home.

"The [industry] data that does exist is not necessarily part of the creative process here, the way it is in America with focus groups and demographics and so on," he tells me during a tour of Studio4C's creative studios and offices, three floors up in an anonymous office building. "You can get numbers for theatrical grosses and DVD sales. But that's not necessarily a part of developing a project the way it might for big studio projects in the U.S., where there's some guy in the office analyzing it based on previous projects."

Arias, a trim, youthful-looking, and relentlessly serious thirty-eight-year-old, occupies a unique role in the Japanamerica story. Not only is he one of the rare foreigners at work in a Japanese-dominated industry, he is also directing his own anime. *Tekkon Kinkreet* is a feature-length version of the Japanese manga by veteran artist Taiyo Matsumoto, known in its American edition as *Black and White*.

Arias has been working on this film for ten years. He does not laugh much. Nor, he says, does he get much sleep. "There's not a lot of money [in anime], but there's a great deal of freedom—as long as you can make the film cheaply enough to break even in Japan."

Arias's boss, former Ghibli producer Tanaka, is one of the few women working in the industry. In fact, she believes she's the only one presiding over a production studio. "When I go to conventions, I have to check my face in the mirror," she says, smiling. "Everyone there is a man so I figure I must be one, too!"

According to Tanaka, the primary focus of the industry, at least for now, is the artistry itself. "Until very recently, market research wasn't really done. There is an industry publication, but we don't now on those details when we work. We think about the genius who will follow in Miyazaki's footsteps."

One of the reasons *Kinkreet* has taken Arias so long to make, aside from the financial challenges, is that he spent three years on another project—*The Animatrix*, released in 2003. *The Animatrix* was produced by Studio4C at the behest of the Wachowski brothers, whose love of anime drove them to conceive of it as a companion to their *Matrix* trilogy. The brothers wrote four of eight short anime films, but left the direction, and production, to the Japanese.

"The Wachowskis just asked me to produce it," Arias says. "I said I didn't know how to produce. They said: 'It's okay, just get whoever you want to work on it.'" Some of the most skillful and daring contemporary anime artists are featured on the DVD. Together with a bonus documentary disk—which, despite its MTV-style, jump-cut impatience, contains intelligent commentary from artists, critics, and scholars from both sides of the Pacific—*The Animatrix* is a rewarding and edifying introduction to the form. Plus, it looks spectacular.

But coordinating it all from Tokyo was apparently exasperating. "It's a part of my life I'd just as soon forget," says Arias, "although it did make this film [*Kinkreet*] possible."

The privileging of the artist in Japan's anime studios is not limited to the medium. It is also not necessarily a privilege based on artistic excellence.

Like most other parts of Japan's highly systematized workforce, the structure of the anime business is more often a matter of hierarchy. You work your way through the ranks, painstakingly performing to expectations. And when it is your turn to rise to the top, you can fly.

The chief animators on any film are involved in the most creative and most critical artistic work, beholden only to a director overseeing the story scene by scene. And the animators have been through it all.

"All the animators here are treated like they walk on water," Arias explains as we pass their roomier cubicles, with superior long-necked lamps and canvases, at the front of the studio. Sample backdrops hanging from thick metal clips are illustrated meticulously, in myriad colors. "They've been working in the industry for quite a while, and now they're the guys who can draw the best and the fastest and make things move. I know a couple of guys who didn't even go to high school. They just stayed at home and drew."

Arias gestures at the empty cubicle of his art director, Shinji Kimura, who worked on the most expensive anime ever, *Akira* director Katsuhiro Otomo's *Steamboy*, released in 2004. "He's now 40, and this is the first feature film he's supervising," Arias says. "It's a lot of work, a long apprenticeship."

It's also a system that can have its drawbacks, both financial and creative.

At Studio Ghibli, a few train stops away and just down the road from 4C, Alpert describes the merits and the pitfalls of Japan's artist-based business. He outlines what he considers the three critical differences between contemporary Japanese and American ways of making narrative art—not just anime, but film as well.

First, the artist is in charge, not the producer who procures the funding, and not the consumer who buys the tickets. Focus groups and demographics are unheard of in Japan's creative industries. No advance research is done prior to a film's release. It lives or dies by the sword of its own merit. Second, the Japanese are both proud and fond of their singular way of seeing things, what artist Murakami branded the "superflat" style: the absence of western notions of perspective and three-dimensional forms. Despite advances in technology, and the increased use of CGI and digital animation techniques, the Japanese cling to their two-dimensional surfaces. Finally, as a relatively poorer country (for years, anyway), the Japanese have become particularly good at doing more with less, adapting to a dearth of resources by econo-mizing and being concise; no less ambitious than other nations, but employing fewer tools.

All of this can result in an approach to the business side of creativity that might infuriate efficiency-minded American producers—all the more ironic, of course, because in many respects, Japan is one of the most efficient and industrious nations on earth.

Alpert proffers film director Akira Kurosawa as an example: While making one of his signature films, *The Seven Samurai*, the director wanted a shot of rain. The film was already difficult to finance, and an entire crew was waiting for Kurosawa to shoot the next scene. Rain machines from the 1950s stood at the ready, but the director refused to use them. He wanted real rain, and would rather eat into the producers' publicity budget to get it.

What Alpert calls "this precision of details" is what he loves about his boss, Miyazaki. He tells a story about the making of *Princess Mononoke* to cinch the comparison:

"When Ashitaka first sees San [the Princess], San jumps on the roof and takes off, and he jumps off and follows her. But when he jumps up, he's slightly heavier, and he hits his foot slightly wrong on the tile and snaps it off, and it comes crumbling down.

"Just a little visual scene like that shows that he's heavier and bigger and just a little bit clumsier, but still powerful. But to do that means that you have to touch the background art. The roof is background art, which is meticulously painted. So to animate it, you have to go in and meticulously repaint all the little bits and pieces and animate them falling from the roof. It's the kind of thing where on a budget, a producer's going to say, 'great idea—but lose it. Too expensive.' But with a director-based movie, the producer might suggest that, but it doesn't really matter. Because

Miyazaki wants to do it. And Miyazaki says: 'The audience is not aware that they notice such details, but they do, and it creates a subliminal atmosphere that they recognize.' "

Alpert sums up his analysis with a reference back to film, the form that first sparked his interest in Japan. "You never have director's cuts of Japanese movies," he says, "because the film you're watching *is* the director's cut."

Of course, there are good reasons why commodity-conscious American studios test the waters of commercial and financial success before releasing titles. Alpert's description of an industry that relies on the whims of its artists reminds me of what aging rock musicians frequently say about record companies in the '60s. To paraphrase: The company executives didn't understand rock 'n' roll, they only knew it was popular, so they let the artists create whatever they wanted as long as they signed with the label. When rock went mainstream, that business model went south.

Nice idea to let the artists have their way. But what happens when you let them run the show, and they are not geniuses?

"There aren't that many directors out there who are that good anymore," Alpert says. "That's the liability of the Japanese system. Everyone's looking for the next Miyazaki. Even Miyazaki is looking for him. But we haven't found anyone."

Except one. In the mid-'90s, director Yoshifumi Kondo made *Whisper of the Heart*, a beautiful and critically acclaimed film that seemed to follow in Miyazaki's footsteps without crudely mimicking the director's signature style. Miyazaki wanted Kondo to take over the Ghibli operations. But three years after *Whisper*'s release, Kondo succumbed to an aneurism. He was forty seven.

Grave of the Fireflies's Takahata is seventy years old. The sixty-five-year-old Miyazaki wants to retire, and has announced so several times. In a spring 2006 issue of the Japanese magazine *Invitation*, Toshio Suzuki, Ghibli's producer, estimates that Miyazaki will make only "one or two" more films.

Miyazaki is still working, but the studio is betting its future on his son, Goro. Nearing forty, Goro has directed his very first feature film, *Tales of Earthsea*, based on the works of American science fiction and fantasy author Ursula K. Leguin.

Mamoru Oshii (*Ghost in the Shell, Innocence*) and Katsuhiro Otomo (*Akira, Steamboy*) are both in their fifties; Shinji Aramaki (*Appleseed, Bubblegum Crisis*) and Hideaki Anno (*Evangelion, Cutie Honey*) are in their late forties. Most of the anime artists whose products have achieved international recognition, from the creators of Pokemon to *Fullmetal Alchemist*, were born in the 1960s.

The pioneers of the medium are getting old fast. In response, the late master Tezuka's studio, Tezuka Productions, opened a facility in China in 1997—partly to capitalize on cheaper labor, but also to train the next generation of artists.

There are many reasons for the dearth of young talent, from the economics of the industry to a lack of inspiration. Alpert believes that the life cycle of the medium is one of its problems. Faced with masterworks by Tezuka, Miyazaki, Oshii, and others, younger animators may feel oppressed, afraid to try anything because it has already been done before, and done brilliantly. There are also what he calls "temptations of technology," the opportunities for growth in CGI and elsewhere. To be a good animator, he points out, "you have to really love the medium, to love film, and to love making things move. That love shows up in the final work, but it's hard to see and feel the passion through too much technology."

Arias agrees that the field of computer graphics has siphoned off younger anime artists. But he also thinks that the medium demands a level of commitment that younger Japanese, raised in the comfort of Japan's boom years, simply do not possess.

"There's a generational aspect to it," Arias says. "We're talking about taking ten to twenty years to make a good animator. I hear a lot of the guys I work with around me who are my age or older basically talking about things like they're the end of the line. There aren't a lot of young people in the world who dream of being animators enough that they're willing to work the way animators work in Japan."

It is this pesky irony that is suddenly vexing professionals throughout the Japanese industry: At the very moment that anime is becoming hip and mainstream in America, its producers at home are desperately seeking a future.

Arias is the American who loved anime style so much that he left home and Hollywood more than a decade ago so that he could create it himself, working out of the very center of the anime universe. He speaks, reads, and writes Japanese fluently; he adapted to the hierarchical Japanese system, working his way up to his current, and in many ways, enviable position: director of a feature-length anime, produced by one of Japan's most adventurous studios.

But when I ask him to peer into the industry's crystal ball, he looks genuinely troubled and his eyes narrow. "I don't see many young faces in animation here—or anywhere—working as traditional animators," he concludes after a long pause. "And I guess my biggest concern is that, before anime takes off in the rest of the world, the industry here will just die out."

3
the business of anime

In only the first decade of this century, the terms anime, manga, and otaku have become common parlance in the American media, no longer explained or defined in parentheses. Anime conventions are held nearly every weekend somewhere in the United States. Chain and independent book, video, and DVD stores devote ever-expanding plots of valuable floor space to products shipped in from Japan. Public and school librarians stock their shelves with anime DVDs and manga paperbacks, the latter on the Harry Potter principle that, as TokyoPop's American founder and CEO Stuart Levy says, "at least the kids are *reading*."

The Mobius strip of interrelations between American and Japanese artists has become Japanamerica in the twenty-first century, when Japan's contemporary popular culture is winding its way into America's awareness. This started centuries ago with Japanese scroll paintings and woodblock prints, some of which both influenced and were influenced by European artists when Japan was officially isolated from the rest of the world, and has continued on up through Disney, Fleischer, and Tezuka—from Kubrick's *2001: A Space Odyssey* to the Yoshida brothers' Sandy Frank-produced *Battle of the Planets*, from the Tokyo-noire mise-en-scène of Ridley Scott's *Blade Runner* to Otomo's *Akira*, from *The Matrix* to the *Animatrix*. The anime-influenced *Powerpuff Girls* and *Hi Hi PuffyAmiyumi* are now produced in the United States, and no doubt many American kids believe that Pokemon, Yu-Gi-Oh, and Naruto are homespun as well—just as an entire classroom of Japanese kids I encountered were certain that McDonald's originated in Japan.

McDonald's, like Starbucks, Hollywood, and the American beef industry, among others, is used to making a good portion of its global income in the world's second largest economy. Hollywood celebrities and directors do not fly halfway around the world every other week on Tokyo promotional jaunts just for the sushi.

But excepting their successes in the automotive and electronics industries, the Japanese have a poorly developed sense of how to profit from their creative output—especially when it comes to intellectual property. The industry that postwar giants Tezuka and

Miyazaki pioneered is, domestically at least, pretty thin on the ground.

"We had a similar problem in the U.S. between 1955 and 1975," says critic Solomon. "The old studios were closing down, and for some reason Disney didn't hire anyone new. The same artists from *Snow White* would make *101 Dalmatians* in the '60s. And this country suffered from a gap where almost everyone in animation was over 65 or under 35. Teachers were lost. A whole generation didn't receive the education.

"I just hope the Japanese learn from us," he adds, "and make an industry that pays more attractively."

On a chilly and rain-soaked Tokyo afternoon, Katsumi and I are crouched in silence over a small table at the back of Akihabara's Maid in Angels café—a place where young men sip coffee stirred and served by the cartoon women of their dreams. Katsumi takes a drink of milky coffee, glances up at "his" waitress and, tongue contorted in concentration, adds another careful stroke to his masterpiece.

He stares at the woman again, taking in her pseudo-gothic French maid costume with studied appreciation. Katsumi is a regular customer, and the costumed waitress has let him stay far longer than his regulation ninety minutes. But now, even he knows his time is up.

"OK, it's finished," he declares with furrowed brow.

Katsumi slides the small sketch book over the table and urges me to flip through its forty-odd pages. As I do so, I find myself watching a superbly crafted four-second animated short of Katsumi himself, roughly hitching up the maid's skirt and having sex with her in the café.

I tell him I think he has real talent.

"So can you pay for the coffee? I mean, I know there's supposed to be an anime boom right now, but I'm flat broke."

Apart from getting another look at his favorite maid, it is Katsumi's near-poverty that has brought us to Akihabara. He is 19 and, according to the buzz in the maid café circuit, he has the skills to make it one day in the business. In the old days it would have been a simpler path: He could have taken a few books of sketches round to the anime mecca in the Nerima suburbs and eventually hustled his way into a studio. He would have worked like a dog, of course, inching his way painfully up through the system while making terrible money, but he would have been doing what he loved.

But the anime industry has changed. Katsumi comes from a new breed of Japanese animator whose approach is decidedly commercial, not emotional. He passionately wants to make anime for a living. But he also wants to be rich.

Having no disposable cash has exposed what Katsumi calls the "super-dumb salaryman-style Japaneseness" of the profession he so badly wants to join. The Japanese anime industry is not going to change to suit Katsumi, so in the back of his mind he knows he will have to change it himself.

Which brings us to the front door of Digital Hollywood, a private university strategically located in the middle of Akihabara, offering young Japanese a unique course that combines digital and graphics technology with the basics of entrepreneurship. To meet the $14,000-a-year tuition fees, Katsumi will have to take out a ruinous loan. But he has come to see the university as the only way to "get into animation as a boss, not a slave."

Japan's decade of slump—roughly 1991 to 2001—produced a generation of creative, entrepreneurial types like Katsumi with values markedly different from those of their parents. The nation's "job for life" guarantee evaporated into the fog of rising unemployment, bank failings, and bankruptcies, and along with it went the faith in a rigid hierarchical corporate system. The term "freeter," a hybrid of the English "freelance" and the German "Arbeiter," or part-time worker, was coined to identify the legions of young Japanese hopping from job to job—and exercising their creativity in between.

"The kids that were coming out of university in the '90s were the first generation in postwar Japan who didn't have an escalator ride to success," notes 2dk's d'Heilly, who founded his company at the very start of the recession. "They learned to think for themselves. They're quick on their feet, they're creative, and they're able to synthesize information and act upon it. And they want success."

Katsumi glances into Digital Hollywood's common room—a colorful den where students loll on low sofas and fiddle endlessly on their laptops. If this were a conventional Japanese university, the kids might be talking about what company they want to join. Here, they talk about the kind of company they want to start.

"It's crazy. The guy who founded this university knows that this is the best way to make money out of Japanese animation. Not actually making animation, but teaching people to do it, and taking their money." He pauses and absentmindedly checks his watch. "But I'm still going to get a loan."

Katsumi's annoyance has complicated roots. As Shinichiro Ishikawa, the president and founder of animation studio Gonzo Digimation Holdings (GDH) notes: "Japan has no lack of creativity—that is not the problem. We have the creative wheel, but we lack the capital wheel. So our cart just spins round and round." From a simple glance at the numbers, this should be the dawning of a golden age for Japanese animation. All but one of Japan's listed animation companies were profitable last year, and others are preparing for their IPOs.

Without any really serious marketing strategies of their own devising, over the past five years Japanese animation studios have nurtured a fast-rising fan base in the United States and rekindled the old passions of European fans of the genre. Feature films like *Spirited Away* and *Howl's Moving Castle* have made their mark in cinemas from Rome to Reno. The Cartoon Network fills about half its airtime with Japanese or mock-Japanese animations; the Akira Kurosawa-inspired *Samurai 7* is a weekly feature on the U.S.-based Independent Film Channel; as mentioned earlier, *Afro Samurai* is set to debut on Spike TV this year, with a feature film to follow.

The domestic Japanese market is even hotter. Four years ago, Japanese TV was broadcasting fifty new anime titles every week; they are now broadcasting eighty. Satellite channels at home and abroad mean that most Japanese animators have around five hits from their back catalog being reared at any given time. In a land where the art form is now at least forty years old, inventory is everything.

The scope of product tie-ins—from video games to cuddly toys—is potentially enormous. Japanese animators have long had the knack for making their storylines an addictive mix of never-ending plot twists. *Dragonball* has been going for twenty years, and the saga shows no signs of drawing to a close. A third generation of seven-year-olds is primed to get hooked.

And technology has opened extraordinary new ways to sell and resell animation. The form has found an ideal home on the screens of third-generation mobile phones, and the anime industry is shaping up as the first to introduce video-on-demand Internet services properly—something that has for many years been sought as the Holy Grail of the media future.

But just scratch the surface a bit, and suddenly the scene is anything but blissful. The global anime boom of the twenty-first century has taken Japan, a country whose corporate culture prides itself on knowing the next new thing, almost completely by surprise.

The people who should have their fingers firmly affixed to the pulse of western pop culture passions are groping around in the dark. Executives of major animation studios have declared that they do not think Gundam is popular outside Japan, and that robots are probably too Japanese to appeal to foreign tastes. They are staggered when a foreigner reels off names like Cowboy Bebop or North Star Ken with familiar ease. And if you come up with something slightly out of the mainstream, like Jin-Roh, they declare you an otaku obsessive.

Every animation professional and/or guru has his or her own explanation for the industry-wide blind spot. The most convincing is that the global interest in animation is not driven by any forces that the industry either recognizes or knows how to exploit. For domestic growth, animators in Japan used to rely on the so-called golden triangle of anime, toys, and video games—a structure of Japanese origin that meant that at any given time you needed popularity of only two out of the three to create and whip up a market for the third. It was effective and predictable and, above all, controllable.

But in the case of the United States in particular, the Internet is playing a colossal role in generating the buzz for and around anime. For Japanese animators, this is new, unknown, and untamable territory, and their response to it has been poor to pathetic. Rather than embracing the fact that there is a new generation of animation geeks cropping up everywhere, and peddling to their every desire, Japan has on this occasion let America dictate its terms.

As a senior board member of Toei Animation remarks with a baffled grin: "It amazes me. For the past two years we have had overseas buyers here all the time! These foreign buyers have so much information about which animes have been popular in Japan, and these are the ones they go for. I have no idea how they accumulate all this information."

Anime presents Japan with a business conundrum that it has never directly experienced in the past, and one for which there is nobody to offer reliable guidance. Japanese industries that have made their names selling abroad have traditionally been manufacturing-based, such as the automotive and electronics industries, and have watched over their products with a neurotic obsessive-compulsiveness. They have crafted the market to suit their exacting needs—and thrown tantrums or imploded completely when the markets shift away from their model. Clearly, they have not provided the anime industry with the help it needs.

For as long as he can remember, Katsumi's talent, he says, comes from shutting himself in his room and just working on his drawings. Going out to maid cafés for live inspiration is a recent phenomenon. He is not a great conversationalist, but he knows there is a fundamental problem with the Japanese animation industry.

Studios, publishers, and distributors should, in his view, be making a lot more money than they are. I ask him to explain.

"I hate most non-Japanese animation, but I love *The Simpsons*. I was watching it on cable and I saw an episode named 'Lisa the Tree Hugger.' For me this sums up Japan's problem."

In the episode (season 12, episode 252) Bart needs cash to buy a Japanese game console, so he takes a job delivering flyers for a Thai restaurant. He is quickly taught martial arts so he can drop off the menus with ninja stealth. He runs sideways along walls, his actions accompanied by staccato swishing noises. At one point the scene freezes, he hangs in the air, and the "camera" does a 360-degree pan around him.

The episode dates back to 2000, a year after the look and feel of *The Matrix* had seeped into viewers' consciousness, and the makers of *The Simpsons* were very adroitly appropriating it into their shtick.

"Think about the origins of that famous scene and style," says Katsumi. "The guys who did *The Matrix* took the idea right out of *Ghost in the Shell* and made millions of dollars. And then it comes back in a circle to animation. But this time, it's the U.S. animation industry, and *The Simpsons* and the Fox network that make all the money. Japan has the ideas. We should make the money. But nobody in our industry has the money smarts to do it."

Japan's lack of drive in taking on the international market merits attention. "There has been a perception that anime is very lucrative, and it is not," says Takazou Morishita, the head of Toei Animation's international division. "So many investors come here and we have to explain the process to them. It is not just a question of milking a cash cow. The number of lucrative hits is very, very small. There are currently eighty anime airing in Japan each week. Maybe five or six or those are making big money," he says.

Ishikawa of GDH is precisely the kind of industry professional Katsumi wants to be: a hard-nosed entrepreneur with a sophisticated understanding of where the international market is heading and the future value of anime as intellectual property. Japan has a social infrastructure—unique in the world—where people of all ages and backgrounds read manga comics. The range of subjects covered in pictorial form is therefore vast and, as anime becomes more popular, gives Japan an edge over the rest of the world that it could retain for decades.

Ishikawa founded his company six years ago on the theory that, in a broadband digital world, animation would be king. He has embraced the international potential of anime, rather than treating it as a surprise bonus.

He believes that the trouble with the industry lies in the Japanese mindset and the dominance of what he calls "emotional money" over "professional money." Professionals, he says, care about returns, and that is what Japan is missing. The troubled times for anime—just when it should be blossoming into a global money-spinner—encapsulate problems that affect not just the corporate world but the whole of Japanese society. Japan, he argues, has a problem comprehending the very idea of intellectual property, and anime represents the first time that the country has really faced the possibility that it may one day be better at exporting ideas than cars and DVD players.

Japan, he explains, is intrinsically scared of investing in the media industry because it is not perceived to be "real." He believes that anime needs to inflate a financial bubble, where investors come to believe in the future worth of intangibles.

"I was at NHK and one of the people there said, 'Don't you think it is crazy that actors in Hollywood get $20 million for a film? We should not get into that in Japan.' I told him that that is exactly what's wrong with Japanese thinking. What we so badly need is an investment bubble for anime."

Ishikawa's criticisms of the media industry have even attracted the attention of the Japanese government. He now sits on a committee of the powerful Keidanren, Japan's business lobby, charged with advising the government on the future of intellectual property and the digital content business. It is currently worth about $12 billion a year, and the government hopes that Ishikawa and the new breed of entrepreneurs can raise it to a $700 billion industry by 2035.

"The potential for anime abroad is huge," says Morishita of Toei Animation. "I think that the spearhead was films like [Mamoru Ishii's] *Innocence*. It's an artistic piece, and the market there has started to understand that anime is a serious medium. The perception of anime as a serious medium for thought and entertainment can only grow from here."

Meanwhile, for the "old" side of the industry, the western anime boom is causing a variety of headaches, but also offering clues for a solution to deeper problems that anime studios have long faced. Katsuhiro Yamada, the chief financial officer of TMS—the company behind *Anpanman*, *Ulysees 31*, and dozens of other classics—is initially negative about the prospects of big foreign growth. His company has no serious presence in the United States and is desperately looking for people to staff its lone Los Angeles office.

"To be honest, we have not worked out what is the best content for the foreign market. I admit that we have not made the utmost effort to get into the overseas market, so now we are doing everything we can to catch up. If we get a demand for ten anime, I think we can do seven or eight, but there is a lack of communication between what they want and what we can provide. I suppose . . . we are in a kind of panic."

As he continues, the story of an industry in the throes of dramatic transformation fast unfolds. Is it possible that the industry's problems with exploiting the U.S. and European anime booms are not terminal, but merely the symptoms of a patient coming out of a long coma? Could it be that the Japanese animation industry is not riddled with incompetence and inflexibility, but is quietly biding its time and changing its form to become as formidable abroad as it is in its domestic market?

Yamada describes the very recent phenomenon of the "Anime Consortium"—an ad hoc collection of producers and investors who raise the capital needed to make whatever is demanded by the market. In existence for about nine years, it is quietly establishing itself as the best way of financing animation. Handled right, the model will give anime companies the previously unattainable ability to say "yes" to any type of request that rolls in from abroad. If NBC wants thirty new episodes of *North Star Ken*, TMS and everyone else in the consortium will not be forced to turn the U.S. buyers away.

Mitsunobu Seiji, president of Studio Hibari, claims that the answer lies in the formation of a union capable of collectively securing favorable deals in the international market. He points to the relatively small U.S. profits made by Nintendo, despite the spectacular overseas success of its Pokemon title. By settling for a flat fee upfront and ignoring royalties, Nintendo, despite its size and apparent savvy, made far less out of the phenomenon than 4Kids, its U.S. distributor. "The animators need to protect themselves and make a change to the system," says Seiji. "We need a union."

Others claim that a union is unnecessary, since the market is already producing solutions. As matters stand, the profits from each consortium are divided among the members according to investment. TMS makes it a policy of being the biggest investor in its various consortia, taking stakes of around 50 percent in each. Freed for action by the consortium model, TMS says it will now start looking into specific products that will play well outside Japan. It has already had some success doing so with *Sonic X*—a cartoon based on the Sega video game character, its biggest seller in the overseas market, and an anime that never actually aired in Japan.

At Rikuentai Studios, president Takahiro Okao has spent a lifetime as an outsider. His love of anime meant that his youth was spent without many friends and, he says, no attention at all from girls. Now on the point of lucrative vindication of his life's nerdiness, he bemoans the fact that although his brand of martial arts and ghost story anime titles have a huge potential demand in the

West, he cannot afford to meet it. "The U.S. filmmakers—like the investment companies and funds—all approach us with offers that are much better than any coming from the Japanese TV companies," he says. "We are very tempted when we get these offers, but there is one problem: We can't make enough titles in so little time."

Japanese anime's popularity in the West now threatens the very source of the quality that makes it so attractive. The new demand has caused a dangerous hollowing out of talent in Japan. "The new generation are 'kamikaze animators,'" says Okao, "who are only taught how to take off and fly straight. Before they have time to become great, they burn out. When I was young, we had three years of training. Now, if you are an in-betweener for more than half a year, people say your career has stalled. There are just too many projects going on at the same time."

Further exacerbating the hollowing out of Japanese talent is increasing competition from Japan's Asian neighbors. Many major studios are quietly outsourcing the more laborious aspects of the production process—especially the in-betweener work, in which aspiring artists painstakingly fill in the cel-by-cel movements that take you from scene to scene. Indeed, Tezuka Productions proudly features its Beijing facility in its corporate brochures and on its Web site.

Lower-cost facilities and labor provided by the Koreans, the Chinese, and Southeast Asians can mean a much wider profit margin, of course, but also far fewer opportunities for work, and cash, for hopeful young Japanese anime artists like Katsumi.

"Nowadays the young ones want a decent income and time to enjoy their lives," concedes Matsuhisa Ishikawa of Production IG, the makers of Ghost in the Shell, a seminal work in anime's success in the West. "And it's not a good idea for us to identify this as a poor industry. People will not join."

2dk's d'Heilly is less sparing in his analysis. "When something works abroad, [Japan's animators] don't see a nickel of it. And most of the producers have done a pretty shoddy job of protecting their industry. And now, here come the Taiwanese, here come the Vietnamese. And the Japanese can feel it all going away from them, just slipping away."

Anyone who has worked in Japan knows not to be fooled by the sterile face of Tokyo's far-flung suburbs. From extraordinary technological inventions to innovative literary works, Tokyo's "bed towns," as they are called in Japan, have proved in many ways the hotbeds of the city's creativity.

In my hand is what could pass as an anime Bible. The glossy Tokyo Movie Shinsha (TMS) back catalog reads like an all-time ranking of Japan's greatest television anime. And on a train from central Tokyo, the journey west allows plenty of time to peruse its 300-odd pages.

They are all there: *Galaxy High School, Ulysses 31, Detective Conan, Lupin the 3rd, Golgo 13,* and *Star of the Giants.* And of course, page after page of *Anpanman*—the longest-running cartoon series of all time, now well past its 800th episode. This is a catalog aimed at the foreign market, a glorious showcase of what should be an industry in the full swing of mega-growth.

Yet the first seeds of suspicion are sown by the faintly skewed English blurb under each of the entries. The science fiction epic *Orguss*, for example, is summed up as follows: "The Story develops using the confrontation between the two organizations, the reconstruction of the world and the human drama created around the hero and his maturing as the ingredients of the story."

Most of the world has come a long way since poorly crafted English by nonnative speakers was funny. Nowadays, and in Japan particularly, it sends a subtle message to potential customers: we care about the overseas market in principle, but not quite enough to pay $400 to buy three hours of proofreading services by a native English speaker. From Kamitakada station, it is a short walk through some narrow Tokyo streets to the offices of TMS: a listed company that, measured by sheer annual output, is the biggest animation house in Japan. But apart from some six-inch stone models of Anpanman on the doorstep, there is little to tell that the squat gray offices are not the headquarters of some failing construction subcontractor. There is Anpanman carpet up the stairs and along the narrow corridors to remind you where you are. But slick it is not.

TMS's Yamada has a complicated story to tell. Fifteen years ago, his company was under the wing of the Sega Games group, but they were taken over by a fur and textile company from Nagoya whose fortunes were plunging steadily toward bankruptcy. After the takeover, the company went through a series of transformations, culminating in 2006 with a declaration of a three-year plan that focuses on anime rights.

"We hold the copyright to most of these"—he says, gesturing at a huge board with dozens of classic titles on them—"and this is how we are going to make money from now on."

As the conversation continues, Yamada's initial misgivings subside. He describes, for example, his company's heavy involvement in Mushi King—an unlikely sounding concept that could represent a twenty-first century resurrection for the old toy-games-anime triangle.

Mushi King relies on the fact that Japanese and now American children have finally moved on from the cozy world of Pokemon and Tamagotchi virtual pets. Japanese youngsters are now in the grip of a new craze: fighting creepy crawlies. The new card-trading, insect-battling video game swept though Japan in just a few months and has converted a generation of six- to twelve-year-olds into aspiring entomologists. And there is now an animation series to stir their passions further.

The Sega-built concept involves small arcade-style game cabinets, of which there are now more than 25,000 throughout Japan, thousands scattered around Europe, and more appearing all the time at Wal-Mart stores and other places across the United States, where parents need to keep their children occupied while they shop. For about a dollar the machines dispense, at random, a collectable trading card with a picture of your new insect and intricate details of its biology, habitat, and dueling skills.

The cards include a barcode. When fed into the same machine, the code starts the fight—against either the computer or another card-bearing human opponent. Similar software exists to let children duke it out on their Game Boys and PlayStations. Because there are nearly 750 varieties of species to amass, the makers explain that what the children are hooked by is the vast range of possible combinations of insect showdowns. The more he thinks about the concept, says Yamada, the more likely it seems that a big animation producer will soon merge with a big video game maker or toy company.

But TMS has tested other waters. Using the consortium model, TMS, Toei, and Sunrise formed an investment pool and created Animax—a satellite and cable channel that broadcasts the back catalog of all three companies, taking in profits on series that would otherwise be gathering dust in their archives.

Nerima is the heartland of the Japanese animation industry—a few square miles of suburbia that has, over the past fifty years, given birth to nearly all the best-known anime titles.

There is a white-hot artistic spark somewhere here, but it is elusive. The place does not ooze the indolent confidence of London's Soho, nor does it have the rough-edged energy of the East Village. It has old women scrubbing their front steps and the smell of wood shavings and glue from small-scale carpentry workshops.

Down a residential side street I arrive back at the studio and head office of Mushi Productions, where I am shown through a chilly corridor and into the meeting room. Windows rattle slightly. Then I am sucked into the broken-spring embrace of a sofa that is probably thirty years old.

Ito, the elderly Mushi president, and a friend and former colleague of Tezuka, sits down with me to explain why his industry needs help. He has run the crumbling anime studio since being handpicked by Tezuka in the 1970s.

Like everyone else who has spent time with Tezuka, Ito toes the official line when talking about Disney. He holds forth on the anime industry beneath framed, yellowing pictures of Astro Boy and Kimba the Lion. But he also has the glint in his eye—that fleeting shimmer, visible in so many corners of Japanese industry, and seeming to say: "We have to respect you, but we do this stuff better than you."

He is quick to point out that even when countries in Europe, particularly France, were nervously putting official limits on the amount of Japanese animation that could be shown on TV, their own domestic animators were quietly outsourcing all their production to Japan.

"What makes Japanese animation different? In the U.S., you use a person to act out a movement then draw what you see. Japan doesn't need all that. Our animators can just imagine the movement in their heads," he says. "I am frankly surprised that the country that produced Disney is interested at all in Japanese anime. Can they truly appreciate what we do?"

But even Ito has to admit that when it comes to funding the future of anime, Japan may turn to the United States for its model. He believes that the fledgling use of anime funds and consortia described above will continue to grow. He wonders aloud whether that will ultimately be good for the industry, leaving little doubt where he stands.

"People who invest in animation will want a return. The concern I have is that only anime that will definitely be major hits will actually get made. There will be no diversity. This particular film I'm working on is too low budget to be worth forming a fund for. But popular themes will be the ones where millions can be made from tie-ins with manga, toys, or video games. They will dominate in a fund-backed-only environment. Nobody will take on the difficult themes any more."

The work Ito is describing is an anime named *Nagasaki 1945*: a grim tale of a doctor working in the aftermath of the second atomic bomb. The entire project was funded by the people of Nagasaki, who believed that an anime would be the best way to prevent their story being forgotten.

"The idea came back in 2003 when people were starting to think about the sixtieth anniversary of the bomb in 200[5]," Ito says. "I went to Nagasaki, where people have a very strong set of antinuclear views, but those people are getting older, so we thought that the timing was good for making this kind of film. People in Nagasaki want this piece to stand as a work of history. It is not the kind of film that the general public is going to be interested in.

"The reason that this is not suitable for overseas audiences," Ito continues, "is that the U.S. sees the bomb as a positive thing. For them, it ended the war quickly. The film is based on what the doctor saw, not the people who died. It is a medical view on what happened, and the message will be lost on the U.S."

Why does he believe that Japan excels at anime? "Because it is easier than making real action. Our ideas are too big. There are a lot of extremely cruel things in the film—lots of terrible scenes—and it is easier to make this in the form of anime."

But the real revelation is yet to come. Ito shuffles ahead of me, guiding me down another musty narrow corridor, from which doors lead off to small animation sweatshops. He opens the door to a dust-floored back room and hastily shoves cardboard boxes and other clutter aside. He snaps on a light to illuminate a matte black piece of aging machinery—a machine that allowed a film camera to be mounted above the animation cels as they were hand-wound in front of the lens.

"This was the machine that Tezuka made *Astro Boy* with," says Ito, his eyes squinting with sad pride. "We tried to give it to a museum, but nobody wanted it."

The Japanese animation industry, after fifty years of commercial and artistic success, and despite its role as perhaps Japan's most important cultural export of the last thirty, has not gained "establishment" status. Its products are iconic nearly everywhere, a few of its creators are lauded as superstars, but the symbolic piece of its inception is an irrelevance—a rusting machine in a dusty room. If the film camera on which *Gone with the Wind* had been up for grabs, it seems likely that some collector would bid thousands of dollars, if not much more, to own it.

Japanese collectors are willing and prepared to pay high prices to own remnants of their beloved pop culture. According to analyses by the Nomura Research Institute, they spend around $4 billion annually, a fact that Japanese corporations recognized forty years ago, exploited domestically, and then, as they do with nearly every other native creation, exported.

But with anime and manga in particular, it seems that so much emphasis was placed upon producing the art that the industry forgot, or was simply too single-minded, to get the word out to potential investors. Now it is being forced to.

4
toy story

By one major metric, the success of toys and games with anime or manga links, anime has already conquered America, and the world.

But in order to appreciate the triumph it is necessary to stop thinking of anime or manga per se as the main products of many anime or manga studios. They are the core products, of course, but not necessarily the most lucrative ones, and certainly not the most successful when it comes to getting a global audience addicted.

Pokemon turned ten years old in 2006. In the decade since its launch, it has made Nintendo and forty different companies around the world a total of $25 billion—the annual GDP of Bulgaria.

So where do the plastic figurines, video games, trading cards, and cuddly toys fit into the picture? The short answer is that they turn the anime industry into something far more familiar to the general sway of Japanese merchandising. But over the past fifty years or so, many have tried to explain precisely what that sway is.

There is a Japanese word that seems to sum up Japan's marketing approach quite succinctly: *monozukuri*, or literally, "thing-making."

Coming from a Goldman Sachs analyst or a journalist attempting to pigeonhole Japan, this would be amateur anthropology. But the word was spoken by the globally revered chairman of Kyocera, one of Japan and the world's most successful electronics and technology companies, and one that has been "making things" extremely well for more than a century.

Let's say that for the Japanese marketing mentality, anime falls squarely into the *monozukuri* ethos: a primary emphasis on tiny details, a love of production for its own sake, and a constant drive to find innovative ways of crafting the product itself.

The ideas, the beauty, the concepts, and the messages are somehow secondary to the finished product. And this is what seduces Japan's hardcore otaku. The relationships between characters and stories are critical, but the most popular background reading on any given anime consistently emphasizes the physical way that scenes came into being—the "behind the scenes" extras.

For an industry in search of profits, anime provides an extremely rich excuse to actually make things. Japanese investors are not altogether happy with the idea of plunging funds into intellectual property. But investing in its profitable side industries—games and toys—is a different matter; suddenly Japanese managers are dealing with something they know and understand very well.

The Pokemon phenomenon can serve as a Rosetta stone for the Japanese anime industry: a critical translation device that unlocked for Americans and Europeans an entirely new language of entertainment.

Pokemon presented American kids with an anime that, because of the universal appeal of its toys, allowed them to decipher Japanese cartoons without cultural or linguistic prejudice. American kids had been playing with trading cards—swapping them, comparing them, and designing battles involving them—for decades. In Rosetta stone terms, the toys and games were the underlying text. The anime style that accompanied them was the "Japanizer" of the theme, allowing their diminutive consumers to absorb the very character of a distinct cultural style.

Each of the major studio bosses that I have visited has sometimes grudgingly admitted that Pokemon was the crowbar that levered Japanese animation back into the United States as a powerful commercial force—and that the Dragonball, Yu-Gi-Oh, and Gundam trends that followed owed their entire acceptability to Pokemon. The vanguard Japanese cartoons of the 1970s had softened the market somewhat, but Pokemon was the driving force that tore it open.

Pokemon delivered Japan to the U.S. market in several ways. First, it familiarized kids with the aesthetic form of Japanese anime—the hairstyles, the big eyes, the stop frames, the complete visual transformation of facial expressions during emotional and dramatic peaks, and the attentiveness to minute details.

In addition, the Pokemon cartoons introduced some of the more complex aspects of anime—the acceptability of the illogical and the ambiguous, the hero's sense of duty above all else, the concepts of child as hero and of unending quest, the undepend-ability of a happy ending, and the fact that no individual episode ever satisfactorily ties up the various and addictive narrative threads.

Pokemon's second trick of "colonization by anime" was the gradual introduction in the week-to-week plot development of new Pokemon characters—a process that was perfectly synchro-nized with the toy merchandising apparatus.

With the Star Wars or Harry Potter toy series, parents were assailed by a single demand for "all the characters and all the play sets." But with Pokemon, they were suddenly confronted with a steady week-by-week demand for whatever new Pokemon had been featured that week.

In essence, Pokemon provided kids not only with the products to desire, but also with an entire strategy for getting them— essentially going straight over their parents' heads and straight into mom and dad's wallets. By hitting parents piecemeal, the eventual aggregate Pokemon outlay would be far greater than that of any other competing toy series.

Perhaps the most critical aspect in all of this, suggest many anime executives, was giving Americans a sense of anime's undying saga—a concept that makes the perpetual marketing of toys inevitable.

Japan's toy giants, Bandai and others, have good reasons for thanking the Pokemon media empire. The Japanese sense of the undying saga, in anime plot terms, remains ambiguous—both optimistic and pessimistic. They may defeat the greatest Pokemon master at the time, but is there someone even greater? They may meet new enemies in that forest, or they may meet new friends. Either way, the audience is hooked, and the fountainhead of commercial opportunity continues to flow.

As noted earlier, Tsunekazu Ishihara, the president of Pokemon Co., told the *Nikkei Shimbun* that the plan has been in place for years. "The basic concept of Pokemon games has remained unchanged since the first release in 1996. But we have always strived to add new characters and upgrade games so that Pokemon fans will never feel they are approaching an end. That is the reason for its prolonged popularity."

He went on to drive home the same message that has become the mantra of the Japanese anime industry as it faces a golden era outside of its domestic market: "[Before Pokemon] Japanese anime had already attained a certain degree of popularity in the U.K., but the U.S. market was dominated by Walt Disney and Warner Brothers cartoons in those days. But Pokemon's strong penetration into the U.S. triggered the massive inflow of Japanese anime. Now American children seem to make no distinction between Japanese anime and U.S. cartoons."

Video game industry veterans—and not just those at Nintendo— also believe that Pokemon represents a turning point. On one level it confirmed that the "killer application" model was alive and well—Pokemon reached the United States at a stage when the video game industry was, as ever, facing another upheaval, and it was a relief to know that at least some of the old ways were working.

If they didn't already have one, kids were buying Nintendo's handheld Gameboy machines just to play Pokemon. When the Gameboy Color was launched, it was Pokemon that drove the sales. The Pokemon game drew American and European kids into a genre of video games that they might otherwise have avoided—suddenly, all those Gundam titles and other variations on the "character battle" theme had tapped a market that had previously ignored them.

As is so often the case in the history of video games, the timing was partly a stroke of luck. Pokemon was hitting the mainstream just as handheld video games were finally reaching a point of technological sophistication where they could properly reflect the complexities of a world in which detailed characters were in conflict with one another.

But perhaps even more important was the visceral experience. Pokemon gave western kids their first proper contact with the naked force of Japan's trend-driven commercialism. They were exposed, without filters, to the marketing juggernaut that the Japanese have learned to live with. Pokemon was translated into English, but that was where its westernization ended.

As Ishihara explains: "Market research conducted in the U.S. prior to the release of Pokemon games found that the characters were too childish to catch the fancy of Americans. However, we decided to introduce Japanese-designed characters without any modifications, which in fact captivated American children. This means that we cultivated demand that had gone unnoticed until then. Pokemon had the power to change the market."

Any foreigner who has held a Japanese video game package, or manga, or bag of candy, or even a can of soft drink in their hands can immediately sense that there is something different about it. Japanese packaging—like Japanese gift wrapping and, one might argue, kimono design—has an enticing compactness that makes one yearn to open it.

Shigeru Miyamoto, the creator of Nintendo's Mario, once described in a single sentence the secret to making a great video game: "In every box, a surprise." The colors are more vivid than we expect, and even the most lurid seem exciting rather than tacky.

In Japanese packaging there is, above all, a sense of the mysterious, the delicate, and the precious—even if it is the cover of a violent, pornographic manga.

The conventional western marketing approach is to treat packaging as a straightforward marketing challenge. How do we use the wrapping to sell more of this product and establish its position in the market? But in Japan, the packaging is an integral part of the product, and probably has been from the product's original conception.

When it came to Pokemon, children were getting a seductive taste of Japan without even leaving Wal-Mart—the colors, the look, the mystery. Gatchaman had been there before, but it arrived freshly renewed in Pokemon. Nintendo had hooked America years earlier, but prior to Pokemon, the boxes for the games were twice the size they were in Japan, and the graphics on them were serious rather than silly.

Pokemon gave America its first glimpse of what Japan could do if it was allowed to get to the children directly, without an interpreter. Kids were probably too young to realize, but Japanese style is sexy, and they were interested.

In April 2005, Hajicho Honjo, president of Ito-en, Japan's largest maker of green tea, gave a rare interview to *The Times's* Lewis. He began with a strange story: His company has long been the market leader in bottled, ready-to-drink green tea—a favorite summer drink in Japan. As more has become known about the health properties of green tea (and as the fear of too many sugary sodas has grown), the U.S. market for Ito-en's wares has expanded. Honjo has opened a shop selling his bottled green tea in New York and is in talks with the likes of Wal-Mart to start stocking the shelves of U.S. supermarkets.

The most popular of Ito-en's teas, Oi-ocha, is actually a stronger brand in Japan than Coca-Cola. Before hitting the U.S. market, Honjo's people did some consultation stateside as well as domestically and came up with a new packaging plan for Oi-ocha on the American market. Oi-ocha became Tea's Tea, and the bottles were striped and dark, rather than lurid and green.

Over a cup of his very best green tea, Honjo confided a secret. Using the New York store as a base in the United States, he had tried selling the bottles of Oi-ocha in the original Japanese packaging, complete with Japanese characters unintelligible to most Americans. "It sold incredibly well," he said. "And I think we may abandon the westernized packaging entirely. Americans seem to just fall in love with the original. Market research is one thing. The real market is another."

This is potentially disturbing news for marketing departments across the United States, who spend their waking hours getting into the heads of U.S. consumers, tweaking everything so that the box of Tide or the bag of Doritos sends all the right signals, both overt and subliminal, to the consumer. Japanese marketers spend precisely zero time thinking about U.S. customers, and all their time thinking about Japanese customers—yet some American consumers still want the Japanese packaging.

Of course, Oi-ocha in New York may prove a regional fluke. The company has put in years of market research in Japan to get at the formula that makes their tea the number one seller. New Yorkers may be the only Americans who get a kick out of a bottle they cannot read.

When it came to Pokemon, though, the market research behind the phenomenon was less visible, but many times more calculated and complex. The anime was the market research, and that was what Nintendo, Bandai, and the others learned in Japan. The viewing figures and the toy sales are part of the same analysis. The characters that work will return for future episodes; the failures do not, making way for the next species.

The introduction of new characters has not always been smooth, however. In 1999, for example, Uri Geller, the famous Israeli psychic and spoon bender, was living in the British country-side. He had been out of the public eye for a while, and a generation of teenagers had barely heard of him. Just before Christmas that year, he had taken a trip to Japan and visited a dedicated Pokemon store. He was mobbed, first by the store staff, then by dozens of Japanese youngsters desperate to get his autograph.

Could he really be that well known among a generation that had never seen his spoon-bending TV antics in the '70s, he wondered?

But instead of thrusting autograph books under Geller's nose, the fans held out one particular Pokemon card. When he studied the card, Geller slowly understood what was happening. Two characters known to western Pokemon fans as Cadabra and Alakazam had rather different names in Japan: "good Un-Geller" and "bad Un-Geller." The characters, whose pictures faintly resembled Geller's face, clutched spoons in their hands and defeated their foes with the "power of the psychic."

Geller, who has repeatedly used the courts to protect his name from any unlicensed commercial activities, planned to sue Nintendo for tens of millions of dollars.

For the kids who bombarded Geller with autograph requests, it must have been an unsettling moment. Here, in flesh and blood, was a Pokemon character. Not a person in a Pokemon suit, but a real Pokemon. Fantasy and reality were mixed spectacularly in one live, breathing package.

How many thousands of autograph hunters over the years must have hounded Sylvester Stallone in restaurants believing that they were meeting Rocky or Rambo? Do the Robert De Niro autograph hunters secretly want him to sign their books "Al Capone" or "Jake La Motta"? Hollywood and other peddlers of mass entertainment make their millions off the confusion of fantasy and reality. When I called Tokyo Disneyland on the hottest day in recorded Japanese history to inquire about the well-being of people inside the character suits, their publicity agent responded: "What people in what suits?"

With his talk of a lawsuit, Geller terrified Nintendo, and the talk may have postponed an extraordinary transition for the Japanese toy-anime axis. Puffy AmiYumi notwithstanding, humans becoming anime characters has not become a major factor in the toy-anime axis, but it might. When *Afro Samurai* hits the movie screens, will ten-year-olds be looking for Samuel Jackson's autograph for the same reason that their Japanese counterparts mobbed Uri Geller—to see a real-life anime character?

The roots of this phenomenon are more than four decades old. Tokyo-based British journalist Leo Lewis of *The Times* (London) recalls a fierce argument with three of his friends in 1982: "We had established that Princess Leia did not really look much like Carrie Fisher, and that Han Solo in the Hoth outfit did look reasonably like Harrison Ford. We were just about agreed that Obi-wan Kenobi looked like Alec Guinness, but were completely divided on Luke Skywalker. As far as I could tell, in none of the figurines that we had—fatigues, X-Wing pilot, Hoth outfit—did the face even slightly resemble that of Mark Hamill. My friend Rory was sure it did—and we came to blows."

The Star Wars toy phenomenon was among the first truly global merchandising events for kids under ten. It created one of the earliest international brotherhoods of children with no Internet on which to compare thoughts, just a few hints here and there, and a subconscious thrill that someone in Paris or Miami might be thinking the same things and arguing about the crafting of figurine facial features.

"For a British kid like me," says Lewis, "it was fascinating to watch E.T. and see Elliot introducing his alien friend to the exact same Star Wars figures that I owned."

But because the Star Wars toy scene was so explosive and so extraordinary, many have mistakenly come to judge it as seminal.

In 1963, the Japanese toy maker Bandai released robot models of Astro Boy, marking the first time an action toy had been based on a character in a television program. There had been plenty of collectibles before, but this was different. Like Kenner Toys' Star Wars figures would fifteen years later, these toys demanded to be played with, not merely collected and fawned over.

At Bandai—along with every other Japanese toy maker—the debate that Leo and his pals and many other kids engaged in in 1982 has been the industrial preoccupation of nearly half a century. Once that first Astro Boy model rolled out of the Bandai factories, character goods would be the future of Japanese toys. And if there is one thing that is instilled early in Japanese children, it is the national obsession with attention to detail. Unlike the U.S. industry, which by 1977 had only Star Wars for a character pantheon, Japan by that time had hundreds of anime and thousands of characters.

Because manga and anime are much more detailed artistic formats than their U.S. and European counterparts, the need to differentiate each toy through physical detail was dramatic. When there are only 100-odd Star Wars characters to model, you can get away with some sloppy modeling. When you have 500 Gundam pilots, you better be precise. Thus Bandai, which has made its fortune with Gundam and Power Rangers, has spent its research and development yen making sure the models look like the anime. This refinement has never stopped.

In April 2006, Bandai announced that it had developed a technology in which a semiconductor laser is used to create toy molds—with a level of detail that comes down to 40 microns. The technology is already in use at the Shizuoka factory, where Bandai makes the Gundam models. If you look carefully at the 4-millimeter pilot (with a magnifying glass?), you can make out his fingernails and the slight wrinkles in his tunic.

The *Nikkei Shimbun* explained: "The Namco Bandai Holdings unit expects to tap demand on the part of enthusiastic 'Mobile Suit Gundam' fans by releasing different versions of products with scratches and bullet holes that follow the progress of the animated television series."

Scratches and bullet holes custom tailored to match each episode of the narrative—this is tie-in merchandising at perhaps its most potent. Children's "nag factor" with parents—their response to a relentless weekend-morning barrage of anime with tie-in toy commercials—is usually restricted to a handful of toys. In Bandai's vision, now intensified with every week that passes, it is not enough to have just the toy from the cartoon: now you have to have a new toy for every twist that the story takes.

Two days after the announcement about the semiconductor laser, Bandai hit the market with another innovation: a new process that would reduce the total period of new toy production to 100 days, or half the industry average. The plan involved a complex reorganizing of the plastic molding machines, the way they are stored and transferred between facilities, and the speed with which a new mold can be rolled into commercial service once the sculptor has done his work.

Within three months from the moment a manga appears on the shelves, or a new anime or film hits screens big and small, Bandai can have the toys in the stores, with more detail than ever before. Never in the history of the toy industry has toy making kept in such close step with the pace of the human imagination.

This highly profitable dynamic is at the center of Bandai's corporate strategy—an ambitious drive to beat Hasbro and Mattel through the soaring global growth of anime, manga, and their related paraphernalia. Having merged in 2005 with the video game maker Namco, Bandai is in an even stronger position to do this; and with the Japanese population now shrinking, the impetus to sell abroad is that much stronger.

Like Sanrio, a company whose Hello Kitty and other characters are turned into toys by the likes of Bandai, Japanese toy makers have become voracious seekers of "characters," and anime represents the most colorful and accessible source of these. It also represents the most effective way of internationalizing toys and expanding the potential market for each new product.

Bandai's president, Takeo Takasu, says it succinctly: "As a chief executive of a toy company I want rights, rights, and more rights. I have very high hopes for the way that countries outside Japan will respond to our partnerships with anime makers, and Gundam in particular is really taking off in the U.S."

"Miyazaki's Oscar gives Japanese animation an even stronger tailwind. Cartoons are very powerful tools because they only need minimal changes to make them localized. We've always had to do a little work to suit international tastes. When the Tamagotchi [virtual] pets died on the Japanese version of the game, they turned into ghosts. American kids got scared, so we had them turning into angels."

Bandai has another, more fundamental reason for wanting to expand toy markets by using anime as a spearhead: "Twenty-five years ago there were 2.2 million Japanese children being born each year. Now that number is down to 1.1 million. If we're only talking about children, it means our domestic market has been cut in half. So of course we look outside. At the U.S., China, Indonesia, and all the other parts of the world."

It is no coincidence that so many of the best-selling toys in the United States over the past twelve years have been Japanese—Power Rangers held the top slot for nearly a decade, and neither Pokemon nor Yu-Gi-Oh has ever been out of the top five.

who's in charge?

Who is really calling the thematic and artistic shots in the anime-toy industrial complex? Is anime merely the "pusher," getting children hooked on a particular line of toys, or are the toys simply tools for enhancing the invasive, addictive power of anime—extending the number of hours a day any given anime is in a child's mind by making sure the characters in plastic form physically surround him?

Hollywood producers have long included scenes that help the crew in merchandising—gratuitous scenes where unnecessarily complex vehicles appear in shot for a few seconds, and whose plastic scale models later retail for $40. Who really dictates the number of new characters that are introduced to anime each week, or the type of vehicles they drive and the weapons they wield?

Mitsunobu Seiji, the managing director of Studio Hibari, is in little doubt that it is the toy companies that have always dominated the anime planning meetings. And he has a strategy for capitalizing on it.

His company is based in Nerima and he heads a local federation of anime studios—businesses that have been in the front line of many of the industry's recent problems. His members are worried by the same things that worry him: an exodus of talent to the video game industry, a hollowing out of genuine artistic talent as the workloads become too heavy, and a sense that anime studios have never gotten rich off their now globally recognized product.

His grand design is to use the Nerima federation as the basis for an anime union—a body that would represent the small studios in collective negotiations with investors and TV networks. It may, he suggests, eventually become the basis of a Hanna-Barbera-style collective whose operations are subsumed into a single company, with the size and capacity to make it bigger than Toei, and better able to meet rising global demand for anime.

"One of the reasons we formed this federation was that the toy makers and the television companies were funding their projects and Nerima just did what it was told. Now we are involved from the planning stage and trying to make it all equal with the toy makers. The weakening of the anime studios has gone too far. Some larger companies have started to think of the anime, toy, and video game businesses as a single export package," Seiji says.

A senior spokesman for the Sotsu Agency, a major producer and distributor of TV anime, leaves little doubt that the toy and video game makers play a central role in every stage of the creative process. He mentions the toy companies at the head of a list of investors for each new project and describes their role in pitching the idea to the TV networks.

But Morishita at Toei believes this is the wrong analysis: "To think of anime as being driven by the toy industry is a misinterpretation. The toy company is part of a process of targeting. Their market research plays into the production of the anime. Our company is actually the outright leader in merchandising around our animes.

"Italy and France were the first foreign markets to be really interested in Japanese animation and become active buyers of it. Golderac was the name the French gave Grendizer [a Robot cartoon figure for boys], and that was in 1978. There is a difference in attitude. The Europeans are comfortable with the idea of animation, while the U.S. has been very difficult to crack because cartoons are a kid's thing."

Morishita, too, sees Pokemon and its followers as the critical catalysts in transforming the American market: "The merchandising links between Yu-Gi-Oh and Pokemon took it to the mainstream.

Essentially, Japanese anime was in the past shown on specialist channels no matter how much marketing effort we put into it. We have six animes running on U.S. TV at the moment on the Cartoon Network and Disney channels. I think we've actually reached the point where we have more of our anime airing in the U.S. this week than we do in Japan."

5
japan's ip problem

If Sony and Matsushita steamrolled Magnavox and Zenith, and Toyota and Honda are racing past GM and Ford, can anime studios like GDH and Studio Ghibli become the twenty-first century heirs to a Japanese industrial tradition?

If they can—or can even threaten to—then their route into American hearts and wallets cannot be the same one that Japanese companies have pursued before. In the past, Japan has been a large-scale exporter of ideas, but only very rarely of what we might call pure intellectual property.

Japan has sold new concepts, and sold them in ways that have gone on to shape daily American lives, young and old. The Nintendo Gameboy, the Sony Walkman, the Bandai Tamagotchi, the Sharp microwave oven are all good examples of this, and prove an important point: Japan generally exports its intellectual property in the form of physical (usually engineered) consumer products.

Even Japanese exports that appear to be idea driven are, at their core, product driven. Images, icons, and concepts—including anime—are often merely purpose-built tools in the hands of their owners. Pikachu and the Red Power Ranger are not so much ideas as they are attractive channels through which to inundate markets with goods.

In a now widely cited 2002 *Foreign Affairs* article, American journalist Douglas McGray defined the concept of what he called Japan's "Gross National Cool": "Japan has made deep inroads into American culture," even though Japan is "usually written off by the rest of the world as aggravatingly insular."

Tellingly, McGray names few examples of Japan's cultural invasion that could be classed as pure intellectual property—in the sense that the idea itself predates the desire to sell a particular product. Japan is extraordinarily skilled at creating characters to sell things. In 2003, CM Databank determined that the most valuable face in Japanese marketing was not the good-looking boys of the pop band SMAP, nor its ubiquitous pop *idoru* Ayumi Hamasaki, nor even Brad Pitt. It was Nova Usagi, a pink cartoon rabbit designed specifically to advertise English conversation schools.

Even the seventeen lines it takes to draw the iconic face of Hello Kitty—whose $1 billion empire became the subject of an entire book by the former *New York Times* Tokyo correspondent Ken Belson—is really just another product marketing channel. In Japan, Hello Kitty sells everything from pork dumplings to coach tours. But she has no story, and even if she did, she has no mouth through which to tell it.

The onset of the digital era has changed the marketing landscape, and the role of anime has taken on a signal importance. In anime, Japan has a massive, exportable IP treasure just waiting to test a theory—Japanese ideas have always been attractive to Americans, and Japan should not have waited so long to sell its anime titles as stand-alone products.

The rise of anime in the United States will be accompanied by all the usual commercial trappings of Japanese cultural advance. Japanese companies are very good at marrying their intellectual property to physical products, and their industrial leaders know better than to miss a golden opportunity. But the digital age means that the cultural flow does not need to come through products. It can arrive on its own, and it is already doing so via the Internet.

The digital age also presents most of Japan with its biggest dilemmas. Product development cycles have been slashed, and the dynamics of manufacturing have been transformed by China. Japanese companies still have ideas, but they now face the so-called innovator's dilemma when it comes to turning those ideas into competitive exports. Things could become starkly challenging if Japan sticks to its old model and does not study and learn from the expansion of anime.

The Internet age presents Japan with challenges so great that it does not even have the equipment to measure their size. By a strange stroke of fortune, anime has accidentally assumed the role of Japan Inc.'s crude sensory system in an increasingly alien business environment—tasting, listening, feeling out the U.S.

entertainment market as if for the first time. Anime is seeking an answer to what may be the most critical question for Japan in the new century: Can its ideas be exported without the gadgetry to go with them? Is Japanese thought exportable on its own?

The growth of anime in the United States will give Japan its first fully functional experience of being an exporter of intellectual property in the digital age. This is uncharted territory. If it gets it right, corporate Japan will have its eyes opened to a new world of opportunity—where imagination, ideas, asymmetric thinking, and raw corporate speed are paramount. If it fails, Japan as a whole could seize upon the attempt as evidence that Japan does not do IP—a sentiment with the power to impede economic progress for years.

Japan has failed several times in recent decades. As Bill Emmott illustrates in his 1991 book *Japanophobia*, Sony's experience with Hollywood is fraught with blunders and lessons for the anime Industry as it now attempts its own brand of colonizatIon.

"Although the Japanese can learn about the entertainment business, they cannot take it over unless American culture ceases to dominate the world music and film markets. The vital ingredient, in other words, is in America. This will be true as long as English-speaking popular culture dominates world markets for film, television, and music, which looks like it will be a very long time indeed," Emmott wrote, adding that Japanese companies have concluded that if they are to stay in entertainment, they have to do things the American way. That means, he added, no penny-pinching—and it entails giving the American managers a free hand—an uncomfortable formula for Japanese bosses accustomed to being in control.

Of course, a great deal has changed in the fifteen years since Emmott wrote *Japanophobia*, but the complexities of Japanese involvement—whether as investors, partners, or direct content providers—in the U.S. entertainment industry remain. The makers of Pokemon feel straightforwardly screwed by the way their IP made the U.S. group, 4Kids, millions of dollars in revenue that should in their view have flowed directly to Japan, and many domestic animators feel the need to have overseas partners hold their hand. They are strangely insecure about the commercial appeal of their own product precisely because they know that their wares are pure IP, and that Japan does not have a long experience as an exporter of products that are not physical.

Here is a rough translation of an excerpt from a report carried on the front page of the Japanese edition of the *Nikkei Shimbun*, May 2006: "Polygon Pictures, the major animation production company based in Tokyo, will produce the new TV animation with the leading U.S. animation broadcasting station, Nickelodeon.

"This collaboration using Polygon's CG technology is aimed at extending their market in the United States. The first production is based on the novel *Akihabara@DEEP*, written by Ira Ishida, a popular novelist of Japan. It is scheduled to start production early in spring 2007, and it will air in spring 2009 in both the United States and in Europe.

"The Japanese animation market has been experiencing very little growth recently. Therefore, this collaboration with Nickelodeon will bring more profit to Polygon, since the company has the copyright of the original work. They expect royalties from selling music, character goods, and games."

There will be more such partnerships, but for how long, and to what extent, is mere speculation. To anyone outside of Japan, it might seem strange that such a relatively minor business partnership should make it to the front page. Japan is feeling its way forward, slowly and tentatively, on the path toward internationalizing its IP.

Unfortunately, there is already evidence that Japan does not understand how to reward its producers of IP. One of Japan's difficulties is its own approach to ideas. Corporate Japan has not, in general, been generous about financially rewarding the men and women of ideas. The women who invented Hello Kitty and came up with the idea for Tamagotchi are not the millionaires they would be elsewhere.

what if anime succeeds?

British journalist Lewis specializes in business reporting. He is also a longtime fan of anime, manga, and video games, the trio that is largely responsible for his decision to study Japan and Japanese.

Lewis's description of his long-anticipated encounter with the man who invented Pac-Man reveals the nature of success in Japan's stodgy corporate hierarchies.

Lewis met Pac-Man's inventor in an unremarkable suburb of Yokohama, but he was thrilled by the opportunity. "What six-year-old can imagine a path in life that brings you to the secret R&D labs of a Japanese video games company?" he now writes in an email interview. "With a single stroke of genius, the man had created the most recognizable icon of the early computer age, shifted the global landscape of entertainment forever, and spawned an industry that is now worth more than $30 billion a year. Of course, I was expecting someone extraordinary to appear."

Instead, the path was down a narrow corridor. A middle-aged salaryman appeared in sandals.

"Hi, pleased to meet you," he told Lewis, shaking his hand. "I'm Toru Iwatani. I invented Pac-Man."

Lewis recalls that "before the meeting, I had trawled magazines, newspapers, and even aging TV footage from the era of global Pac-Mania. Iwatani had figured, though not excessively so, in the descriptions of the furor. These were different days, and the story was always about the creation, not the creator. It was never stated openly, but it was somehow important to Namco in particular, and to Japan in general, to shield the world from the revelation that this extraordinary phenomenon was the work of one man, rather than a team. There are musicians who have penned one-hit wonders and live the high life on their royalties. Despite the great value of his work, there is little to suggest that Iwatani leads the good life."

Lewis describes the room: a tiny space decorated only with a few plaques, a couple of yellowing photographs from the good old days, and a cheap stuffed-toy version of Pac-Man—the gluttonous hero of the most successful video game of all time.

Toru Iwatani, now fifty, granted Lewis the rare interview because his signature character, Pac-Man, had just turned a quarter-century old, and he wanted it recorded in the pages of *The Times*. "It was as if he was getting some dirty secret off his chest," Lewis writes. "Something that was like a burden for him."

Iwatani recounted to the journalist the entire story of Pac-Man's invention. At age twenty-four he ordered a margherita pizza at a Tokyo restaurant chain called Shakey's. When he took up a slice, he noticed that the pizza had a profile: a round head and an open mouth. That, notes Lewis, was only the official birth of the Pac-Man image.

"The whole thing actually started with me walking around games arcades watching how many boys were playing, and the fact that all the machines were about killing aliens, tanks, or people," Iwatani recalled. "Girls were simply not interested, and I suddenly had a motivation for my work: I wanted game centers to shed this rather dark, sinister image, and it seemed to me that the way to raise the atmosphere of any place is to entice girls to come in. The whole purpose of Pac-Man was to target women and couples, and get a different type of player involved.

"I was wondering what sort of things women would look for in a video game. I sat in cafés and listened to what they were talking about: mostly it was fashion, and when they'd exhausted that subject, they talked about their boyfriends. Neither of those were really the stuff of good video games, so I kept listening. Next they started talking about food—about cakes and sweets and fruit— and it hit me: that food and eating would be the thing to concentrate on to get the girls interested."

"He was basically setting the record straight," Lewis says. "He couldn't say too much sitting in front of the Namco PR guy, but you could feel his resentment. He has to know that if he were anywhere else in the world, he'd be on the golf course, never needing to work again."

Lewis's take is that there was an official (*tatemae*) version of the Pac-Man story and an unofficial (*honne*) one. Iwatani had lived through the Japan Inc. era of the 1980s—the days when devotion to your company was par for the course, and the company was expected to offer you lifetime employment.

That has largely changed. Japanese inventors have now begun suing their former employers for proper remuneration—most notably, Shuji Nakamura, inventor of the blue spectrum light-emitting diode (LED), fundamental to the development of DVD players. Nakamura moved to California and, realizing what he was owed, saw another kind of light. He sued Nichia Corporation, and in 2004 he won a settlement of $188 million.

And there are younger Japanese who have entered the IT sector and earned their millions by the time they are in their thirties. Devotion to a company is no longer its own reward.

Iwatani and his team were given a lot of freedom to pursue their own ideas, but as Lewis notes: "It was only because his bosses were too ignorant of the emerging video game industry to do anything other than trust a twenty-four-year-old otaku's instincts."

The anime-otaku connection is revealing. At the time, both anime and video games were characterized by minimal but attractive details in two-dimensional formats.

"The four iconic ghosts—each with its own different color and movement pattern—were based on *Obakeno QTaro*, the famous anime ghost, which Iwatani sketched for me on a scrap of paper," Lewis continues. "But there's also an anime connection in that Pac-Man brought character to the world of video games. The player was no longer in control of a car or tank or gun or tennis racket, but instead you controlled a 'person'—a figure that existed in his own universe and was surrounded by other characters, also full of life. And the ghosts were both evil and cute, and Pac-Man was both innocent glutton and uncompromising carnivore. Each screen could be completed, but the quest itself never came to a close."

The game also appealed to primal emotions: hunting, feeling panic and greed, and the thrill of revenge. Its power pills transformed prey into predator. And you would wind up eating your enemies.

"From very early childhood I have always loved practical jokes and playing tricks on people," Iwatani told Lewis. "I love doing things that provoke a reaction. It gave me so much joy to know that over the entire world, people were affected by my game. Even if it was only one page in their lives."

Lewis was most startled by Iwatani's resignation in the face of the millions he should have earned. "You work for a company all your life in Japan," Iwatani told the reporter. "I want to emphasize that I received no particular bonus for inventing that game. People think I made a fortune and that I'm a rich man. I'm not."

Japan has—sort of—begun to realize that Iwatani's experience carries an important lesson. Iwatani may have lived in an era in which company service was its own motivation. His twenty-first century counterparts on the creative side will not be so easily neglected.

Companies will be left to deal with that side of things, but it is significant that the Japanese government has also realized that it could be doing more with its ideas. Starting in 2003, it began belatedly to acknowledge that phenomena like Pac-Man, Mario, Pokemon, and Gundam are how millions of outsiders see Japan.

2dk's d'Heilly says that the government's sudden emphasis on culture was prompted by anime's success—but also by *gaiatsu*, or foreign pressure: "There was a radical shift in cultural policy here around 2003, with the government investing an enormous amount of money into cultural agencies. There was inherent interest from the anime, which reached a point of maturity or a new kind of position with the success of *Evangelion*, which was much more easily absorbed into international youth culture. The other reason the culture industry decided to recognize contemporary culture was because of a little article about 'gross national cool' that came out in 2002."

That little article was the essay by American journalist McGray discussed earlier. In it, McGray argued that Japan was "reinventing itself" as a global power, no longer focusing on its manufacturing trades, but focusing on cultural products instead. He used Harvard professor Joseph S. Nye's term "soft power," or the capacity to get what you want through attracting others, rather than forcing or paying them, to explain how Japan's popular culture was putting others under its sway, and doing so peacefully.

"That article was referred to a lot, and 'soft power' became a catchphrase on politicians' lips," says d'Heilly. "A lot of money was given to develop it. It was a tipping point."

Yuasa agrees: "Cultural policy shifted exactly one year later. That story was the piece they were looking for, waiting for, to validate their notions."

Perhaps, runs the new thinking in official circles, it might be a good idea to exploit rather than ignore.

In May 2006, Japan's foreign minister Taro Aso found himself in the common room of the Digital Hollywood University in Akihabara—the same university in which my friend Katsumi wanted to enroll. Aso was there to unveil a government campaign in which Japan will improve its image abroad by promoting its pop culture, including the establishment of an international prize in manga.

The pop culture campaign will start in 2007 and will be promoted directly through Japan's global embassies. Diplomats whose days were once spent arguing over dollar-yen exchange rates with Washington hard-liners, or negotiating sugar tariffs with the Brazilian agriculture ministry, will now be promoting anime on the Japanese taxpayers' yen.

"Japan boasts newer forms of culture that have a high degree of appeal," Aso announced. "This would be pop culture, including anime, music, and fashion, among others, and the Ministry of Foreign Affairs is going all out to market it."

The audience of young animators looked stunned.

If the Japanese government is about to start a global sales marketing campaign to sell its ideas and imagination, there are two entities whose reactions matter most: the United States and Japan.

So far, the approach has appeared benign. American kids love *Totoro*, and their parents love it too. Dragon Ball has a lot of fighting, but its violence is really no more brutal than the antics of Tom and Jerry. The kid wants a Gundam robot—it is just another toy like the rest of them. So what if geeky teenagers like that weird manga stuff and a few adults get their kicks from anime porn? It remains, for the moment, a relatively containable phenomenon.

The potential conflict could arrive when Americans soon perceive the deeper impact of Japanese cultural exports. Anime is beginning to dictate the look and style, and even forming the bases, of major Hollywood movies. Anime and its ambiguous, sometimes apocalyptic plotlines dominate the leisure hours of millions of children and young people. Anime is teaching kids that not every story has a happy ending—a lesson whose timing parents might prefer to control themselves.

Isn't it somewhat subversive for young Americans, reared on the Hollywood worship of the individual, the cult of meritocracy, and a deep suspicion of social communism, to hear the heroine of *Ghost in the Shell* say to her colleague, "What's true for the group is true for the individual"?

Culture with that level of following can have a hard time in the United States when Americans begin to become more aware of its influence. Lewis told me of Iwatani's bafflement when discussing the banning of Space Invaders in several southern states in the 1980s—allegedly because aliens are not in the Bible, and because of the game's violence towards them.

The rhetorical savagery and Toyota-smashing protests of American anti-Japanese sentiment in the 1980s and early 1990s has largely subsided, and the old particulars of Japanophobia have dropped away. But are new ones, focused on Japan's pop culture invasion, preparing to take their place?

It is tempting to ponder how long it will be until Fox News covers a public meeting where one special-interest group or another decides that manga and anime have gone too far and, à la disco records in the 1980s and Dixie Chicks CDs in this century, makes a towering bonfire of *Tri-gun* comics and *Sailor Moon* DVDs.

If (or when) that happens, the likely triggers will be the standbys: sex and violence. The siege mentality amid perceived cultural invasion will not be sophisticated enough to realize the truly subversive nature of anime and manga, and the critically important

1. Kinetic Tokyo
© Joan Sinclair, PINK BOX

2. Women and Children
© IN THE EVENING OF A MOONLIGHT NIGHT, Digital Juice, Studio 4°C

3. The bombs bursting in air
© MIND GAME Project, Studio 4°C

4. No boundaries
© PRINCESS ARETE, Studio 4°C

5. A new way of seeing
© ETERNAL FAMILY, Beyond C, Studio 4°C

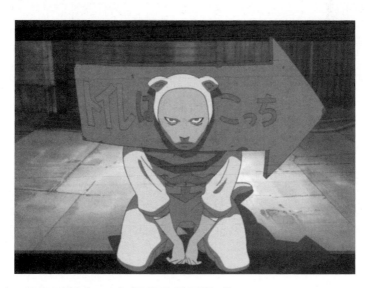

6. Cosplay Central (sign reads "Toilets This Way")
© ETERNAL FAMILY, Beyond C, Studio 4°C

7. Cool Japan, Mushi-Shi
© Yuki Urushibara/KODANSHA-MUSHI-SHI Partnership

8. Otaku-tailored PATLABOR THE MOVIE: LIMITED COLLECTOR'S EDITION
© 1989 HEADGEAR/BANDAI VISUAL/TFC

9. Japan's trauma, Manga's muse
© NAGASAKI: 1945, Mushi Productions

10. Treating Wounds
© NAGASAKI: 1945, Mushi Productions

11. Afro Samurai: The Future of Hollywood?
© TAKASHI OKAZAKI, GONZO

12. Peach Fuzz
© TokyoPop

13. Sailor Moon
© TokyoPop

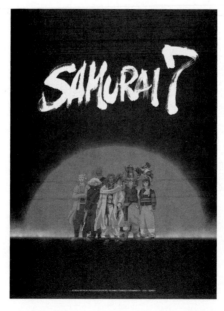

14. © 2004 Akira Kurosawa/Shinobu Hashimoto/Hideo Oguni/Mico.GDH.GONZO

15. Future shocks
© DIMENSION LOOP, Studio 4°C

16. Protean Hentai
© Joan Sinclair, PINK BOX

relationship between the two. It is a uniquely powerful relationship: two distinctly well-packaged products with a combined
ability to addict millions of users.

Despite its relative inexperience selling pure IP around the globe,
Japan understands deeply the commercial power of ideas.

Since the dawning of the Internet age, and the opening of the
digital era, much American business commentary, analysis, and
public debate has centered on the mantra that "content is king."
This is accurate, but perhaps a good deal more so than the United
States properly acknowledges.

The phrase is often employed by commentators as a nod to
the success of America as a provider of global content. But
today, Japanese anime and manga are reinventing the nature of
content's reign.

Ultimately, TV over the Internet, massive plasma screens, the
fastest broadband connection, the most powerful games console,
and the latest high-definition disk player are of little worth if there
is nothing good to watch, read, play, or listen to. That is why producers make films like *Titanic*, games like *Tiger Woods Golf*, and TV
series like *24* and *Lost*. Content is king because it is the most
important consideration in the design and success of any new
technology. It is the policy maker, ruling over supply.

But in the Japanese sense, content is a different sort of king. It is
the direct controller of its subjects—ruling over their demand.

Anime is producing quality content at a time when quality is
becoming endangered by advances in technology, which are out-
pacing attempts to control and even monitor distribution.
And anime greets the American viewer with an enormous back
catalog, a supporting volume of content. That is what makes
it such a potentially powerful force in the digital age—when quality content will arguably become even more greatly prized, as

discriminating audiences have access to nearly everything, and want only what is good.

Watch any type of anime across its many genres—giant robots, cyborg police, intergalactic romance, samurai showdowns, school baseball, teenage alienation—and you are welcome to fall in love with the genre of your choice, and pursue much further its long list of titles. In each genre there is plenty more. And if and when you manage to get through the best of them, there will be thousands of manga exploring the same terrain. That is the addictive power of the anime-manga axis—not only can it hook you on something seductive and habit-forming, but it also can connect you with suppliers hoarding a massive stash.

The sum effect of this is that anime and manga provide an increasingly content-hungry world with something that Hollywood, for all its inventiveness, has not yet found a way to approximate: the chance to deeply, relentlessly, and endlessly immerse yourself in a world driven by prodigious imagination. It is a world with no ceiling limiting the number of times you may visit and explore—because the flow of its content is so steady.

The Japanese entertainment industry, perhaps unwittingly, has realized something fundamental about what contemporary audiences want from fantasy, whether it is science fiction, sports, or romantic fantasy. They want the action to take place in environments that they can know in detail, and repeatedly visit. Consider the successes of *Lord of the Rings* and the *Harry Potter* series, whose offshoots include video games, novelizations, playing cards, and so on. Yet their various manifestations pale next to the myriad variations of the Pokemon media empire, or the variety of tie-ins currently available to the Japanese anime/manga fan that its industry hopes to export successfully to America.

The modern younger viewer, in particular, is no longer satisfied with a few brief glimpses of a new world, or the idea of an invisible book describing every nook and cranny and explaining why things are so. They want to see it all for themselves—and they want to be a part of it.

You may adore the futurescape scenery of *Blade Runner*, but there are only so many times you can watch the same DVD and the same scenes. But if you love the futurescape environs of *Ghost in the Shell*, you can reimmerse yourself in it through dozens of anime and hundreds of manga. When Hollywood has spun off TV series from its major science fiction movies, like the anime-inspired *RoboCop*, they have been disappointingly short on the proliferating details the brave new otakus crave.

What Hollywood tends to offer may be compared to serial love affairs, rather than the deeper commitment and endless discoveries of anime and manga. Thirty-four-year-old Patrick Macias, Mexican-American author of *Cruising the Anime City* and a forthcoming book on Japan's female otaku, traces his obsessions with anime and manga to his Sacramento childhood, where he finally stumbled upon a medium that implied a future.

"Anime and manga, which I got into as a teen, seemed more artistic and sophisticated, even as they could be enjoyed simply as bizarre sex and death stories," he says. "When it came to the level of imagination and artistry, Japanese pop culture just seemed so ahead of the curve. It contained a sense of the future. Other than *Star Wars*, America was stuck in the same cold war mentality it had been in for decades. All we kids had to look forward to was crap like space shuttles and bigger telescopes. No wonder kids like me became mad for transforming robots."

If you are a fan of *Spider Man*, the only option you have is to wait three years for *Spider Man 3*, or perhaps explore other Hollywood superhero films. Once you are through with *Hulk, X-Men*, and a handful of others, your otaku obsession has effectively reached its finale. But with anime and manga, the axis is nearly endless.

For *Super #1 Robot* author Matt Alt, thirty-two, the content entry point was robot toys. He was raised in Maryland, in a suburb of Washington, D.C., and his encounter with the worlds of anime and manga came early. "When I was three or four years old," he says, "I became obsessed with robots—C3PO, Robbie the Robot. And when I was about five, someone in my family gave me this two-foot-tall Japanese robot. In Japan, the shows were made to sell the toys. It's the other way around in America. But the thing is, kids love to be exploited. My robot was made of hollow plastic, and it had Japanese characters on its stomach. I was just fascinated. I was a voracious reader as a kid, but while I knew the *katakana* characters were obviously trying to communicate something, I couldn't get it. Even my mother didn't get it. But I did get that these Japanese people were out there, and that for them, these shows were accessible."

The existence of Japan as the real country from which anime and manga fantasies issue provides yet another layer of content ripe—and actually available—for discovery. It is similar to the appeal of decades-old British rock bands for contemporary teenage Americans: You can find back catalogs of the material itself, then board a plane and visit the country from which it came.

"Fans of *Lord of the Rings* can't go to Middle Earth, and *Harry Potter* fans can't get to Hogwarts," says Macias. "But you can save up your money and book a flight to Tokyo, or just dream about it while savoring the endless details and depth of history."

By comparison, even the greatest Hollywood films—many of which heavily influenced Japan's most innovative anime creators—are short bursts of genius.

Production budgets amount to hundreds of millions of dollars. Teasers and trailers are shown months in advance of release dates. The stars do the circuit of talk shows in the weeks before the movie premiers, uttering slight variations on the same themes: how exciting it was to film such-and-such a scene or work with such-and-such a director, how difficult, but rewarding. In the end, we get about 110 minutes of fantasy. The ratio of publicity to actual content is embarrassingly disproportionate.

Of course, Hollywood continues to produce scenes that are often visually astounding and memorable. The futuristic New York in *The Fifth Element* is but one example. But the scenes are relatively short-lived. We have no time to drink in their beauty, to let our eyes seek out every detail of this strange world, or to imagine ourselves living there—because the clock is ticking and the action has already begun, and we have to concentrate on its real-time assault.

In this respect, manga, and even anime, returns us to the more user-friendly format of the novel. We can decide when to start and stop, and we have the time to luxuriate in an imagined world.

Star Wars is mentioned by all, whether Japanese or American, as the one exception that proves the rule, and it is no accident that it was the springboard for one of anime's critical American invasions: Frank's *Battle of the Planets*.

The global success of the film series owes as much to the supreme richness of its environments as it does to saga itself. Six films paid careful, lingering attention to the sights, sounds, dirt, and dents of their settings, and focused equally hard on the micropolitics of the "galaxy far, far away." There were also comics, books, toys, and a host of other media through which fans could reenter the Star Wars world and explore it for themselves.

Through all of its many guises and spin-offs, *Star Wars* provided multiple, detailed points of access to a fantasy world, and held out the constant promise of more to come. Anime offers a similar promise. Its titles often deliberately leave endings hanging because its maker plans on delivering more to come—even if it issues from a slightly different source.

Miyazaki's Studio Ghibli is the major anime exception. Largely because of Miyazaki's abhorrence of merchandizing schemes (he doesn't even like home video, says Alpert; he prefers that you watch his films once through, with no pauses, in a movie theater). Ghibli has adopted the Hollywood approach to the content business: You can adore the womblike embrace of *Totoro*'s tree cave, but only for a few minutes, unless you rewind the VHS or DVD source. Your only way back to that world—or to the rowdy saloon of a spaghetti western, or to the dark menace of Don Corleone's study—is through rewatching the few seconds that appeared in the original film. Ghibli adheres to a paradigm we associate with western nations: the cult of originality.

japanophilia/japanophobia

Japan's relationship to foreign Japanophilia has always been complex—perhaps even more so than its response to Japanophobia.

Japanophobia, whether expressed by westerners or Asians, can be and often has been dismissed in fairly simple terms. American Japanophobia was essentially a combination of two instincts.

At the level of tracts like Michael Crichton's *Rising Sun*, there was ill-informed jealousy and fear at the speed of Japan's economic growth and its ability not only to compete with U.S. industries, but also possibly to destroy some of them—as is happening in the auto industry today.

Slightly more sophisticated was an irritation that Japan was able to succeed with a style of capitalism that was not a direct copy of its American counterpart. Chalmers Johnson, a professor at the University of California, San Diego, and head of the Japan Policy Research Institute, wrote in his best-selling 2000 book *Blowback* that what disturbed the United States most about Japan's success was that at the height of the cold war, it had found a third way between Soviet and American theories of the market: "The Japanese had invented a different kind of capitalism—something no defender of the American empire could accept. It was therefore assumed either that the Japanese were cheating, or that they must be headed for a collapse."

In Asia, the Japanophobia was more visceral, resulting from a hatred of its old imperialist aggressor and a jealous fear of Japan's rapid return to economic health.

In both the American and Asian cases, Japan got the point without much trouble: these feelings of Japanophobia, while unpleasant to endure, were all perfectly natural and had clear causal links.

But it is when foreigners started to admire and love Japan that the understanding grew muddled. Japanese may love to show you their culture, but when you show that you are genuinely entranced and addicted, they are thrown into turmoil.

One response is a sort of baffled bemusement: "You really like sushi? You really like manga? How come you drink so much Pokka canned coffee?" There is a touch of Japan's inferiority complex—a surprise that their tiny and weather-battered culture could be so fascinating to those who have not lived under its strict rules. But I have often wondered whether it is not, in part, a mask of self-deprecation. Beneath the wide eyes of surprise lurks a more subtle expression: "Of course you like our culture. It's great."

The recent success of Japanese intellectual property (exported cultural ideas) suggests that others are appreciative as well. Young Japanese are especially aware that people outside their country can be hooked on cultural ideas that, like Sony Walkmans in the 1980s, bear the proud sticker, "Made in Japan." Space Invaders, Pac-Man, Pokemon, Power Rangers, and Hello Kitty are all multimillion dollar evidence that is hard to ignore.

Japanophilia is sometimes treated with contempt by those who find foreign interest in the tea ceremony, sumo, or *ikebana* merely superficial: signs of curiosity, sure, but nothing more, and nothing that will allow for an understanding available only to the Japanese themselves. A more academic-oriented Japanophilia is relatively straightforward, and because it is institutionalized, is often easier for Japanese to accept. Art historians, academics, economists, and other experts in their fields have entirely legitimate reasons for their interest in Japan, and it is clear to most Japanese that a culture as ancient and distinctive as their own should appeal strongly to those who study it.

But with a few notable exceptions, Japan's reaction to the American anime boom has been characterized by considerable confusion. The sluggishness of the major anime studios to recognize the opportunities, and the absence of concerted efforts to control digital copyrights in a manner similar to the RIAA, is striking. Some studio professionals that I visited—including the producers of commonly downloaded titles like *Ayane's High Kick*—were genuinely astonished to learn that foreigners were interested in their products at all. Others wearily played down the interest, brushing it off like so much oppressive hype, a passing fad that would doubtless soon fizzle out.

6
strange transformations

Any watcher of anime or reader of manga is accustomed to the conventions of its urban settings: the jumble of skyscrapers mashed together at sometimes bizarre angles and stretching endlessly into the deep horizon, the oppressive and impersonal sameness of every block in *Akira*'s futuristic neo-Tokyo, the narrow back alleys and circuitous side streets into which characters disappear—or have dramatic, yet isolated, confrontations. Like many anime heroes and heroines, the city seems to metastasize into a monstrosity, a marvel of the artists' imaginations.

But those who actually visit Tokyo, Yokohama, or Osaka are likely to realize that the city scenes in anime are not that much of a stretch. Urban layouts in Japan are a far cry from what our minds have absorbed if we are coming from New York or London, or, for that matter, Beijing or Shanghai.

Bombed-out Japanese urban centers rose from the ashes of World War II at record speeds, and in some respects, they look it: an ancient temple and garden in the shadow of a fifty-story sky-scraper, adjacent to a dilapidated two-story hulk of wood and rusting iron, leaning to one side and missing a door; nameless streets dotted with fluorescent-lit convenience store chain out-lets, all of which look exactly the same; a dead-end alleyway with a leafy grove on one side and a garish pub, an Italian restaurant, and a family cemetery on the other. Not a few western commen-tators and tourists, especially from older generations, find Japan's urban hodgepodge decidedly ugly.

On a micro level, the contemporary Japanese city is like a maze, or a Gordian knot never completely untangled. On the macro level, it is either a vision of a thrilling, almost incomprehensible mass landscape—or terrifying proof of the human capacity for unchecked development, cancerous construction. Japan's river-banks are encased in concrete, as are most of its shorelines, many unnecessary walkways, and the now notorious public works pro-jects: country roads leading to nowhere. Japan's bucolic tree-lined streets are rare and treasured.

The New York skyline at night is one of our world's visual won-ders. It is elegant and poised, possessed of itself: a vision of the city as a grown-up, dressed in finery for the evening with its millions of

125

twinkling eyes. Seeing Manhattan at night from the window of an arriving train, or through the porthole of an airplane, is like looking upon a jewel: proportionate, elegant, proud.

By comparison, the Tokyo skyline is as dense and unreadable as a computer chip. Its circuitry is embedded in the Kanto plain, an expanse of flat land that is notable in Japan for its vastness. Seen from space, Tokyo is the brightest urban region on our planet.

The computer-chip analogy is apt; strolling past Tokyo's unmarked streets and chaotic mix of shops and signs can feel a lot like surfing the Web. Everything leads to something else, but it is difficult to control what you see and where you end up. And as with an explorer in cyberspace, among the first things that an explorer in Tokyo encounters amid the abundance is pornography.

It may be useful to think of concentric circles to understand this. On the outer ring, Japan's cities rose quickly, so real estate went to whoever could afford it, and zoning laws were virtually unheard of. On the next ring, in the absence of the West's Judeo-Christian black-and-white dichotomies, Japan is—as Tezuka's Shimizu notes—a gray zone between China and America, a zone where morality is less dualistic. Thus selling an erotic comic down the street from the gates of a temple is not such an affront.

Finally, context. Japan's identification and strict demarcation of *honne* means that you need not feel guilty in that realm—so long as you are not harming someone else. You need not feel guilty, for example, if you masturbate in front of your computer, or read a pornographic manga on the train ride home.

But this can be difficult for an American to assimilate, at least at first. Whether we like or disdain pornography, we are taught that it ought to be hidden away, cast out of sight under the bed, in the basement, or at the back of the closet—or else at the very bottom of a pile of "respectable" periodicals. And even our most dissolute cities have red light districts, identifying the repositories of amoral/immoral images and behavior and isolated as much as possible from Main Street or City Hall.

New York's Times Square used to be one of the red light districts, until more profitable entertainers like Disney and Sanrio were invited to invade "the crossroads of the world." Now Times Square is allegedly harmless. But is the selling of corporate fantasies of the good life any better than selling fantasies of good lust?

In America, the answer is a resounding yes. Expressions of lust threaten to tip the applecart of order in every society; but in ours especially, where such expressions are so often equated with manifestations of real violence, they become doubly dangerous.

Hentai, the word most commonly used in the West to refer to anime and manga porn, is not the word used in Japan. As the translator Lisa Kato tells me: " 'Hentai' is a scientific term that can mean 'metamorphosis.' When insects go through 'hentai,' we mean a transformation." The word's two kanji characters, *hen* and *tai*, roughly mean "strange metamorphosis/transformation," and the Japanese do use the word "hentai" to describe an individual with a perverted fetish, like a flasher, who may undergo a strange transformation indeed.

In a twist of Japanamerican irony, the Japanese refer to porno-graphic anime and manga with words borrowed from English: "porno anime" and "porno manga," or else "ero anime/manga," with the meanings (erotic) quite obvious. In the West, we return the favor by reconstructing definitions lifted from the Japanese: "hentai anime" and "hentai manga."

Perhaps both cultures feel the need to exoticize and make more foreign that which can so explicitly display our horny *honne* fantasies. But I like the western use of "hentai," for it gets at the visual and imaginative properties that make pornographic anime and manga so striking: the sudden yet fluid transformations of characters and scenes.

In live-action pornography (lots of which is also made and consumed in Japan), the slow fade with quivery screen is a convention meant to tell us that we are entering into fantasy or flashback, both of which serve the same function of whisking us away from the humdrum present-tense scenarios required to establish some sense of story. The same convention has long been used in daytime soap operas, though the fantasies there are generally more romantic and sentimental than erotic.

The quivery fade has been mocked for many years in comedic films and TV programs like *Saturday Night Live*, and mocked by viewers wishing to show their superiority to the genres by poking fun at this low-tech dream weaving. In the age of broadband Internet access, in which streaming and downloadable videos provide instant access to a disorienting array of fantasies, the quivery fade seems almost quaintly generous: a patient guide holding your hand as you leave the here and now.

Anime, of course, has never needed the convention because the course is reversed: You need to believe in anime's humdrum present-tense scenarios first. You must accept, for example, the realism of the illustrated world of *Akira*'s neo-Tokyo 2019, rebuilt from the ashes of World War III, and its biker-gang delinquents before you can enter into the fantasy of the coming global apocalypse—and of the more visceral, personal apocalypse that takes place in the hero Tetsuo's grotesquely mutating body.

But once you do embrace the anime world, the form seems ideally suited to pornography's headlong rush into fantasy, where other mutating bodies perform different functions entirely.

tentacle porn

I arrive a few minutes late at Akihabara station, but Hoshizaki does not seem to mind. It is a warm afternoon and he is engrossed as usual in the pages of a *yakuza* (Japanese mafia) manga story. When I greet him, he slings his backpack over one shoulder and continues reading. He does not look up.

A few awkward seconds pass. Finally, I reach down and he allows me to turn the book around so I can see what is happening on its pages.

A heavily tattooed man (*yakuza* member) is stripped naked and strapped to a wall. His torturer who wants information is slumped on a nearby chair, lighting a cigarette. Thick dollops of sweat form on the victim's forehead and ooze down the sides of his face. I turn the page.

A buxom woman in a G-string slinks into the room and begins to massage and then to suck the naked man's penis. Just as his excitement ripens, she pulls away.

A knowing smile plays over Hoshizaki's face as I try to turn the next page. In the following frame, the woman produces a small poisonous snake from a bag. The snake sinks its fangs into the man's penis. His face contorts, elongated by spasms of pain. "Bet you didn't see that coming," says Hoshizaki dryly.

Nope, I admit.

"See, they wouldn't put that in an American comic, would they?" he remarks, leafing through to another story, in which a woman is raped by a werewolf.

"Everyone thinks we have some kind of rigid society here, and sometimes that is true. But you know, people in Japan are not embarrassed by their imaginations."

I am meeting Hoshizaki, a self-confessed otaku of pornographic manga and anime, because he told me that he was worried. I have known him for a few years, and when he discovered that I was researching the hentai forms of anime and manga, he was desperate to prevent me from presenting the subject cloaked in what he calls "western prejudices."

In his *tatemae* day job, Hoshizaki works for a company that makes office-issue coffee machines. In his *honne* free time, he is buying, reading, or sketching his own hentai manga. He likes many of hentai's manifold subgenres. But in general, he prefers the more inventive material—the illustrations of what would be barely possible in the physical world.

"The Japanese obscenity laws used to be a lot stricter, so what you find is that a lot of the most imaginative stuff comes from older artists' attempts to get around them," he says.

His comments remind me of George Orwell's 1941 essay, "The Art of Donald McGill," in which the author praises a then representative form of obscenity, the comic erotic postcard, which was being either overlooked or taken for granted in his modern Britain. Orwell writes that the cards' expressions "only [have] meaning in relation to a strict moral code."

Hoshizaki explains Japan's codes, and how the manga and anime artists respond to them: "Basically, you can directly show girls being made love to by anything that isn't an actual cock. That's the key. So that's why artists make all these stories involving demons with hundreds of tentacles, or trees with branches that do naughty things. It's imaginative and mythic, of course, but it's also necessary."

In some respects, this is a revelation to me. Many of my friends in the United States have asked me variations of the question, what's up with that weird Japanese porno anime? Hoshizaki has given me at least one part of a complex answer. If you can't show humans fornicating, you need to broaden your palette.

"There's a whole genre referred to as tentacle porn," says the historian Charles Solomon, trying to sort out American reactions to the more risqué anime and manga finding their way into U.S. markets. "They show women being raped by demons with various appendages. Yet I know Japan is one of the safest societies for women in the world—violent crime against women is relatively rare in Japan. But the Japanese consume a great deal of anime, manga, and related materials that we [in America] find overly violent."

For us, perhaps, the image of a male's genitalia penetrating a woman's genitalia suits our sense of the actual, however much we try to keep it from our children. But if you are an artist of erotic activities, and you are barred by your government from illustrating the actual—why not try a tree branch, or a tentacle?

"[The Japanese] seem to have these fantasies about this stuff," adds Solomon. "But they don't actually make their culture unsafe for women. In most American cities, women are far less safe on the streets than they are anywhere in Tokyo."

Incestuous rape, urbane salarymen seducing simple farm girls, samurai-era gang bangs, and so forth. For Hoshizaki, they are yesterday's porn. Unless the artistry is particularly superb, he has only passing interest.

"To be honest, a lot of it is just boring porn in cartoon form," he says. "It's just there to serve an immediate purpose, and a lot of it is terrible."

As an example, he cites the fifteen-odd pages of cartoon porn that appear in most of Japan's twenty or so weekly tabloid news magazines. Knowing their audience well, their stories usually involve a salaryman feeling nervous, inadequate, or sick around a beautiful female staffer. Events conspire to make them have sex, and the hero's anxieties are instantly replaced with a highly aggressive, healthy sexual drive.

"It's the Big Mac of hentai," concludes Hoshizaki.

I have seen bits of Hoshizaki's encyclopedic collection, and it is certainly not dull. He has a particular passion for a branch of futuristic manga in which large-breasted schoolgirls are raped by robotic machines, then forced to become part cyborg themselves. Another genre he likes involves good and evil alien fairies who fight an internecine war in the brains of young girls and boys, forcing them to become insatiable nymphomaniacs, violent sodomites, sporadically impotent—or superhumanly well endowed.

Hoshizaki takes me to his favorite anime and manga specialist shop, on the sixth floor of an Akihabara office building. It is crowded and noisily kinetic, like the insides of a pinball machine, with the same sort of multimedia barrage you get in any Japanese video game shop or entertainment or convenience store.

Amid the onslaught, I notice a new Japanese video game prominently featured, called RapeLay. On the cover is a hand lunging toward two obviously underage CGI-animated schoolgirls, who peer at their unseen attacker with stricken looks of terror.

The game is a first-person-perspective simulator, exploiting recent advances in graphics technology and computer animation to give the player an ultrarealistic rendition of his chosen rape scene. As with many of today's video games, you, the player, control everything, from the vigor of the attack to the tone of the victims' pleas for mercy.

Before I explore the game further, I find myself imagining how a newspaper or wire article about such a game might be headlined in the United States: "Sick Japanese video game makes fantasy rape a reality."

But, of course, it does not make the fantasy a reality, any more than tentacle porn subjects real Japanese women to rapists who look like octopi or attack with tree limbs. It is just a superior rendering of a fantasy, and a better, more engaging game.

"I knew you would pick up on that kind of thing," says Hoshizaki before I have said anything to him. "This is precisely why foreigners jump to the wrong conclusions."

Stuart Levy, CEO of Tokyo Pop, describes a similar scenario. On the verge of a major investment deal, he took his two would-be American financiers on a tour of Akihabara.

"They were great guys, and we'd talked a lot," says Levy. "But one guy was a really observant, strict Jewish guy, and the other guy was Catholic. The Catholic guy knew a lot about manga. He was a little younger and had grown up in L.A. But the Jew knew nothing.

"I made the mistake of taking them to a shop that carried hentai manga. I just wanted to show them how much manga there was here. So I took them there, and we went on the floor that had the real hardcore stuff, and they turned completely white. One of the guys was actually black. But they both looked like ghosts."

He did not close the deal.

Hoshizaki spends some time finding me a representative selection of hentai manga. These include *Life is Peachy?*, in which a girl about eight years old entices her older brother to have sex with her, and *No Mercy*, in which a schoolgirl unleashes a satanic curse, grows a penis, and is reduced to tearful, screaming agony by the molestations of a multitentacled demon.

At the cash register, the cashier chats with me openly and amicably. He nods at my selections and informs me that *No Mercy* has made it to the top of the current month's all-Japan hentai manga charts. If I elect to sign up for a discount point card, he says, I can get 10 percent off the price of whatever title occupies the number one slot next month.

Sitting with Hoshizaki in a café later, I leaf through *No Mercy*.

"Isn't this just a little disturbing?" I ask, pointing out the ferocity of the demonic-tentacle/weeping-schoolgirl rape scene.

"They're just pictures," he says. "And anyway, you've seen it before. Hokusai did a woodblock print of a pearl diver being raped by an octopus more than two hundred years ago. It's the same thing. And you people," he adds, "put Hokusai in art museums."

The hentai branch of anime and manga is neither representative of the whole medium nor especially original in its core output. Bestiality, rape, and incest have been used as fictional or artistic themes since writing and illustration began.

But western prejudices and impulsive moralistic responses are a hindrance to analyzing the more complex and sophisticated aspects of the genre. Taken as a whole, hentai products reveal a critical lesson about the Japanese approach to entertainment of all types.

On one level, as Hoshizaki suggests, Japan worships the freedom of the human imagination and is notably unashamed if that imagination is fully expressed and widely consumed. Adult sex with schoolgirls is illegal in Japan, but an outright denial that the thought ever crosses some people's minds is patently absurd.

So long as nobody is being hurt (which they are not, for example, by the existence of a game like RapeLay), Japan is intensely serious about the pursuit of happiness, even without having it mentioned in a formal declaration of independence.

Imagination, runs the unspoken Japanese argument, is a sign of our humanity, whether it is expressed apocalyptically, erotically, or through multitudinous species of Pokemon.

"When I think about western pornography, it's not terribly interesting," says author Susan Napier. "But I find the Japanese stuff very imaginative, and I wonder, why do they need more than just the obvious? *Playboy* and *Penthouse* have their comics, but they're not well developed. Usually four panels, and that's it."

Napier adds that it is not just men who revel in the freedoms of Japan's hentai fantasies. "Think of the ladies' comics. Some of them are about rape and torture, and having weird things put into one's body and exploding inside. They're not read by just men, by any means. A lot of girl's [*shojo*] manga are read by everybody, and there are fantasies of coed couplings in some of them."

To explain the culture behind hentai, Napier recounts her first trip to Japan more than thirty years ago, when she was startled to discover what she calls Japan's "more porous boundary" between imaginary other worlds and reality.

"I began to see there was more occult stuff in Japan, occult manga in the '70s, flying saucers, *aum shinrikyo*," she says, referring to the cult convicted of Tokyo's 1995 subway terrorist attacks. "One of my friends is a translator of Kyoko Izumi, a turn-of-the-century writer who genuinely believed in ghosts. You know, in the West we have Cartesian dualism. But in Japan, you don't have to believe in one thing or another. You can believe in multitudes."

Despite its ritual, social, and ceremonial etiquette, Japan has produced a popular culture that travels admirably light when it comes to religious-based moral compunction. Noncontextualized clips from supposedly outlandish Japanese TV shows have been used to entertain American and British audiences for decades. In the 1980s and early '90s, there was an underground market for VHS imports of such shows; now they appear on the Internet, and they continue to be shown on Spike TV and other cable channels. Many are crass, many are straightforwardly degrading, but it is striking how many ideas for reality shows, game shows, and even global phenomena such as *American Idol* have their origins in Japanese prime time.

Hentai serves as a kind of guinea pig test of the Japanese imagination: We can watch and analyze its development for the simple reason that everyone knows and cares about sex. By contrast, not everyone knows or cares to know about mobile battle suits, biker gangs in futuristic Tokyo, alternative histories of the Tokugawa period, the mechanics of intergalactic steam trains, or the emotional hang-ups of cloned schoolgirls. Within these broad genres, the displays of imagination on the part of the authors and artists can be varied and stunning. But in the context of something that is already premised on a highly imaginative theme, it is often difficult to tell which particular piece is more or less innovative.

With representations of sex, the raw mechanics are fairly limited, so the extent to which the artists exercise an imaginative flair is far more visible. For example, I have a clear idea of how the naked man and woman pictured in the first scene of a hentai manga titled *Do Ya* might behave when left alone together. But the subsequent appearance of a scene depicting a ghost-possessed lascivious tree with penis-shaped tendrils gives me a deeper sense of how far the artist will divert from the basic tableau. And when the protagonists begin to speculate philosophically about the origins of the tree's libido-rich personality, it becomes harder for me to dismiss the story as conventional porn. It is definitely erotic. But the phrase "going all the way" takes on an elaborate new meaning.

The most attractive promise of manga and anime producers is that there will always be more to discover. The inventory of *bishonen* or *yaoi* manga in which beautiful androgynous men fall in love with each other—immensely popular among women twenty-five to thirty-five years old—will not easily be exhausted. *Yaoi* is an acronym for the phrase, *Yama nashi, ochi nashi, imi nashi,* meaning, "no climax, no ending, no meaning." Its female artists and writers are free, soap opera style, to keep their sagas revolving around love and romance. Anime about dunderheaded policemen, teenage sports prodigies, and school bullies will continue to be churned out by domestic studios. Whatever the subject matter, the industry keeps its promise to deliver undying sagas to its audience.

The same dynamic is true of hentai. But the fundamental difference between *Life is Peachy?* and Pokemon is this: A quest to collect monsters in Pokemon is already imaginative enough on its own, while *Life is Peachy?* has to work extremely hard to make a familiar theme, sex, interesting.

cause and effects

The strict separation of fantasy and reality stands out as one of Japan's strongest features in a century where both are being blurred by the forces of globalization and technology. But it is also paradoxical: One part of a culture is comfortable with Napier's more porous boundaries between the real and the imagined, another part imposes strict boundaries on both the real and the imagined. Finding where those boundaries are, where the lines are drawn, can mystify an American, or any non-Japanese, to whom the culture might seem at once both a pleasure dome of guilt-free perversions and a hyperprim overpopulated dystopia.

The expressions of bafflement, skepticism, and weariness that greet me when I tell seasoned anime/manga industry professionals about the rising popularity of their products in the United States are colored by another emotion: concern.

Japan's cultural norms are centuries old, and for more than two of those centuries, those norms were honed and cultivated in nearly complete self-imposed isolation. The awareness of context is almost like a sixth sense, built densely into the complex dynamics of social interaction. So while it may be acceptable for a commuting businessman to open his hentai manga portraying violent scenes of rape and molestation, that does not mean that the packed train is all *honne* all the time. As anyone who has visited Japan knows, a crowded commuter train is by necessity among the most stiff-shouldered, etiquette-laden environs in the land. You twist your body uncomfortably, awkwardly tilt or simply abandon reading materials, place your bag at your feet or on the racks above the seats, and utter "I'm sorry" or "excuse me" *really?* numerous times—all in an effort to survive the journey without offending anyone.

Therefore when you take some of Japan's more provocative domestic creations (hentai) into a less-codified American culture that bans Space Invaders, is outraged by a pop star's naked breast at a sporting event, and impeaches a president for his sexual peccadilloes, you may have every reason to feel a little worried. As many industry insiders confided, they are risking more than just a blemish on their nation's reputation abroad. They are risking lawsuits.

When I return to the United States from Japan, I am initially relieved by our comparative freedom from social rules. I no longer need to excuse my lame behavior or apologize for my awkwardness several times a day; I don't need to bow low before my superiors or elders, or express misgivings for suddenly entering a room. Sharing a crowded elevator does not automatically require standing in lock-kneed respectful silence; I can chat with the person next to me instead, without seeming weird or intrusive.

But that freedom also makes America more chaotic, unpredictable, and sometimes unnerving. Waiting at passport control in

JFK after the thirteen-hour flight from Tokyo, I have more than once seen shoving matches break out over positions in line, loud cell phone gabbing, and other perceived slights.

So we impose the order, the rules and regulations, elsewhere—or at least we try to. Our skylines are shapely and poised, the neighborhoods below segregated into zones of higher and lower behaviors, their streets named and numbered. On any one of those streets, if I had the opportunity to purchase a can of beer from an unmonitored vending machine (not that this is an option in the United States) and, as many Japanese construction workers do, sip from the open container along a public sidewalk, I could be arrested.

Our Puritanical roots, together with our need to simplify and clarify the social codes for immigrant arrivals, cast pornography of any nature into the dark side of American life. If our fantasies revolve around Judeo-Christian categories of good and evil, heavenly angels, and hellish demons, then expressions of unfettered lust and violent longings must invariably be perceived as evil.

In America, per capita statistics for incidents of rape and other violent crimes really are a pressing problem, far exceeding the number of such incidents in Japan, as Solomon notes, and threatening to destabilize the society in which they occur.

The University of Tokyo professor and literary translator Motoyuki Shibata analyzed the differences between the two cultures as we discussed manifestations of violence in American and Japanese literary works: "I think it was Nathanael West who said that in America, violence is idiomatic—which means to me that violence is everywhere . . . an almost necessary by-product of American individualism, which can always turn into the every-man-for-himself kind of chaos. If you push individualism far enough, maybe it explodes." The repressive nature of Japanese culture may keep such explosions limited to the imagination, he said. "If you look at Katsuhiro Otomo's anime, like *Akira*, the violence is more movielike, and it seems to come mostly from the author's imagination."

The ubiquity of sexual violence in real American culture has made us, in turn, take a repressive approach to the culture of our imaginations.

A comparison of train station magazine kiosks in Tokyo and New York is revealing. In Tokyo, pornographic manga and photographic publications are clearly displayed amid the many fashion, entertainment, sports, leisure, and news magazines. The furled daily newspaper headlines are arranged in a way that mirrors the chaotic vitality of the city's mishmash of neon signs and storefronts. In New York, the pornographic titles are largely relegated to the back, some of their covers hidden behind cardboard so that only the cover model's face and bare neck are visible to passersby—marginalized, like the city's strip clubs and other "adult" establishments.

There are exceptions, to be sure: New York is not Nebraska. But by and large, we expend a great deal of legislative energy and money trying to stuff the proverbial cats of our sexual or violent imaginative fantasies into a dark and distant bag.

fritz and garfield

Consider the fates of two animated American cats, Robert Crumb's Fritz and Jim Davis's Garfield.

Fritz grew out of the underground comics movement of the 1960s, of which Crumb is probably its best-known artist—and Crumb is also his own best-known creation. A cartoonist character named "R. Crumb" gradually took center stage in the artist's work. The 1994 documentary *Crumb* and the 2003 feature film *American Splendor* nearly a decade later cemented his fame as an unwitting and unlikely American celebrity, and the artist moved to France to escape the attention and demands on his time.

But Crumb's first cartoon character was a cat named Fritz, a countercultural collegiate male with a voracious sexual appetite, as well as the will to act on it. His appearance in publication in the mid-1960s marks a hentai-like moment in the annals of American cartooning: an adult-oriented narrative giving free expression to the darker fantasies of its artist and readers. With its emphasis on urban density, sophistication, and contemporary attitude, the quotation, attributed to Crumb, describing Fritz in 1968's *R. Crumb's Head Comix* sounds somewhat like a tagline for a contemporary anime or manga, hentai or not: "A sophisticated, up-to-the-minute young feline college student who lives in a modern 'supercity' of millions of animals . . . yes, not unlike people in their manners and morals."

Fritz the Cat would later reach a wider audience via director Ralph Bakshi's 1972 film of the same name, the first animation in American history to receive an X rating. As in many henati anime and manga, illustrations of the penis appear frequently through-out the film, which defied expectations and became a critical and commercial success.

But although there are stories of U.S. pornographers subse-quently attempting to introduce animated sequences into their live-action scenarios, and of Hollywood producers considering developing the medium further, Fritz's legacy is largely relegated to the underground, cult, or alternative movements in American popular culture.

Bakshi would go on to direct *American Pop* and *Coonskin*, among others, both of which influenced American directors and audiences by suggesting more sophisticated possibilities for animated films. But it was his animated version of J.R.R. Tolkein's *The Lord of the Rings*—intelligent, but primarily targeting children—that had the most impact on the American main-stream, though only by proxy; Oscar-winning director Peter Jackson's live-action adaptations of the same series—incidentally rife with CGI animated scenes—took over from Bakshi's earlier animated version. Bakshi's other projects, however groundbreak-ing in their day, remain the stuff of midnight movie showings or campus screenings.

Fritz's future was not helped by his creator. Over artistic and financial differences with the director and producer of the film, the iconoclastic Crumb ended his *Fritz the Cat* print series during the year of the film's release, by having a leggy female ostrich stab

Fritz in the neck with an ice pick—after Fritz refuses her sexual advances and physically assaults her.

At the time, Crumb was not yet exploring violently sexual material in explicitly human realms (his signature human caricatures, like Mr. Natural and R. Crumb, would appear later). The characters in *Fritz* were anthropomorphic males and females, and while they may be "not unlike people in their manners and morals," they do not undergo the fantastical physical transformations and metamorphoses, or the transitions between reality and fantasy, from which hentai gets its name.

Still, Crumb's *Fritz* was the first to bring to American comics the graphic sexuality and violence that we find in Japanese manga and anime. The very year Fritz arrived in U.S. theaters, the saga died. That cat was back in the bag, to be tightly sealed away.

The cartoon cat Americans have embraced instead, so much so that his image is a fixture of American advertising, film, and TV, is Garfield. Not strictly aimed at a childhood audience, the *Garfield* narrative is notable for its childlike preoccupations—food, sleep, laziness, and minor practical jokes in small-scale power struggles with the parent figure, the cat's human male owner, an irredeemable and unremarkable nerd named Jon Arbuckle. Tellingly, the series is almost entirely devoid of sexuality. While a pink, gap-toothed female cat named Arlene occasionally pines for Garfield's affections, he ignores her and focuses on his own needs. Owner Arbuckle is a hopeless bachelor, apparently incapable of even the most fundamental romantic interactions with the opposite sex, and hardly obsessed with exploring the mysteries of womanhood and sexual desire on his own. Arbuckle is a nerd, but he's no otaku.

On television and in film, Garfield's voice is that of adult male actors, the former TV host Tommy Smothers and Bill Murray among them. Unlike the squeaky-sounding Mickey or baby-quacking Donald, and far from the yearning and philoso-phizing adolescents of anime, the actors do not convey the vocal aura or rhythms of younger characters. Instead, the Garfield char-acter's voice is that of a glumly apathetic adult American male, and both his predicament (laziness and boredom) and his most common dilemma (deciding between restraint and gluttony) are childlike only in that they are part of a stunted narrative.

It is worth reflecting on author Frederik Schodt's description of a manga-obsessed and "more autistic" Japanese culture—which then produces manga and anime that explore every facet of an active and vibrant world of the human imagination. By contrast, *Garfield*'s cross-demographic appeal in America may partly result from its presentation of a comparatively autistic world, where Americans may see expressions of some aspects of their lives, or their fantasies.

None of the above is meant as a critique of the artist Davis's cre-ation, which first appeared in 1978 with a set of intentions and a context vastly different from that of Crumb's *Fritz*. But if *Garfield* is at least partly indicative of mainstream American perceptions of an adult cartoon, then the appearance of hentai anime and manga in the United States presents a potential jolt to those per-ceptions, one that could eventually stem the tides of their advance into U.S. minds and markets.

According to Dr. Lawrence Eng, one of the most hotly debated topics on anime Internet bulletin boards and in related chat rooms is the prevalence of pornographic imagery in Japanese animation—and whether or not it ought to be subject to U.S. censorship. Indeed, as Eng notes, the question of whether an illus-tration of any sort can actually be pornographic at all lies at the heart of the matter. A pornographic photograph or live-action film inevitably involves the participation and objectification, willful or otherwise, of at least one real human being. But an illustration, however graphic, offensive, and/or violent, is an expression of the artist's imagination.

Using the Motion Picture Association of America as a model, the import publishers TokyoPop created a rating system for their manga publications in the United States, with appropriate age ranges stamped onto the book covers. The system was soon adopted by Viz and other publishers and importers, and it has so far satisfied all but a handful of American librarians. "They trust us," says TokyoPop's Levy.

But books, as we are constantly reminded, are old media. They are physical, and if they are published by a company, then they can be and usually are edited, vetted for inaccuracies, checked for potential offenses. The same can be said of DVDs, whose rapid rise as an entertainment technology may well be accompanied by an equally rapid dive. Many tech gurus and anime fans have echoed versions of the same prognostication: It is all going to the high-speed Internet.

Type the word "hentai" into your favorite Internet search engine and you are immediately presented with millions of hits (more than twenty-six million, by my most recent count), many providing free downloads and/or streaming clips of pornographic anime, very few branded with age-restrictive warnings. The titles, graphics, narratives, and far-out fantasies come straight from Japan, thousands of miles from most Americans, yet accessible through the click of a mouse. You can download them onto your iPod and watch them wherever and whenever you choose.

The transglobal community of American, Japanese, and other otaku has undergone its own hentai-like transformation. Among other mutations, there are now "fanslations" (translations of manga and anime into other languages, most commonly English) and "fansubs" (subtitles by fans). The most popular, the most striking, or just provocative anime titles across a variety of subgenres can be found on the Internet within days of their release in Japan.

As Napier writes, whether we like it or not, our physical world is rapidly losing ground to the technological and the virtual realities in which we coexist.

Like the modern Japanese city, the Web is a comparatively unmonitored, unfiltered domain. Your search for a Starbucks in Tokyo may lead you to the sex shop next door shamelessly displaying the latest in discount dildos. Your online search for more of the magical *Totoro* anime spell that quells a child's tantrums may send you to the hottest titles in tentacle porn. But unlike the Japanese metropolis, the Web is part of no ancient indigenous culture to draw the contextual lines of propriety for you.

Their failure to come to terms with this has meant that countless Japanese anime artists and producers are losing financial and artistic control over their creations, leaving some of them facing bankruptcy, others rushing to consolidate, and a few planning to produce membership pay sites to protect their copyrights. But our American failure to come to terms may result in moral outrage—and draconian crackdowns that could severely damage the future of Japanamerica.

7
cosplay and otakudom:
the draw of diy

It is not just the artists and producers of manga and anime who have engaged in the transcultural cross-pollination of Japanamerica. As fans soon discover, if their passing interest blossoms into a passion, both mediums have the seductions of the do-it-yourself (DIY) factor: anime/manga fandom is participatory, and communal.

This is similar to the DIY attractions of early rock 'n' roll, or better yet, punk rock—both of which inspired millions of teenagers not only to buy the CDs, T-shirts, and other band-related paraphernalia, but also to make and play the music themselves. The garage band was born, and tape trading, bootlegging, and Deadhead-style fan tours—in which the band's fans literally follow in the footsteps of their heroes' concert tours across the country—ensued.

If there is a rock concert equivalent for fans of anime and manga, it is the anime expo or comics convention. The annual Japanese industry event, the Tokyo International Anime Fair, used to be the largest by far. But America is rapidly catching up, according to historian and critic Solomon. "A few years ago, when I started going to Anaheim [the California site of North America's largest such expo] it was only a fair-sized group showing up for a single day. Now it's something like several thousand visitors, and it runs for four days." Anime Expo 2006 featured the largest number ever of participating anime producers, manga publishers and artists from Japan, and broke its own attendance record set the previous year—by only its third day.

The Tokyo Fair is, like any other trade fair, principally an opportunity for industry players to show off their wares to members of the media and to domestic and international distributors. It, too, is a four-day event, but it is open to the general public only during its final two days; the first two are devoted to industry insiders and those with press passes. More than two hundred companies host booths and exhibitions, and with film previews, costumed performers, and a dazzling array of visuals, it is very colorful. Walking through the maze of brightly lit booths featuring massive mecha robots with gleaming metal surfaces or equally gigantic doe-eyed, big-breasted anime heroines—all of them glaring and

147

beckoning—is a dizzying experience. I felt something akin to a narcotic high, making me stay much longer than I needed to.

But while the Tokyo fair's performers and models may be costumed, its visitors are not. Cosplay—dressing up as anime and manga characters—is prohibited.

The exact opposite is true in the United States, where brochures, newspaper articles, and Web sites advertising the events strongly encourage cosplay, sometimes featuring photos of costumed participants from previous years, often, like their Japanese counterparts, in elaborately detailed getups and makeup. But unlike their Japanese counterparts, they are parading around in a very public forum.

The manner in which Americans have imported cosplay (which, like virtual pop bands, is something I never imagined taking hold in the United States) is revealing, and reminiscent of the U.S. approach to karaoke. In Japan, singing karaoke (which literally translates as "empty orchestra," for the band that is not there) is done in relatively private settings, as Coppola shows us in *Lost in Translation*. Japanese enter private rooms, usually in a group of friends or colleagues from the office, sometimes with fellow bandmates trying to work out harmonies, occasionally alone to practice singing solo. Immediately after you enter and are seated, the menus are passed around and a member of the wait staff appears to take your order: usually a drink and an assortment of Japanese bar foods like soy beans, fried noodles, and tiny pizzas.

The effect is more like being with friends in an American living room—and singing with them. You can dim the lights, adjust the volume, reverb and pitch on the karaoke machine, or just kick back and watch the rapid-cut music videos on the giant screen, made specifically for karaoke. You can sing along with your friends, or sit and quietly enjoy the technique of a skillful singer, or discreetly plug your ears.

The size of the room, the proximity of those around you, and the participants' willingness to risk humiliation among one another all conspire to make karaoke in Japan a decidedly intimate experience—effectively conveyed by Bill Murray and

Scarlett Johansson, whose characters share a deep and longing stare while the former croons (or croaks) Roxy Music's "More Than This."

Karaoke in America is usually sung in a bar larger than any standard Japanese karaoke room, amid strangers, with doors opening and closing, glasses clinking or crashing to the floor, and loud discussions underway. Often you are standing on a stage, facing the tables and an impromptu and distracted audience. It is a vastly different kind of pleasure, though the imported word and the fundamental activity are the same. In America, land of open spaces, you are out in the open, performing for the masses.

There are public cosplay events in Japan, but aside from outdoor promotional campaigns in Akihabara, they are often of a limited size. You are more likely to see a few individuals—usually young and usually female—strolling the streets of Harajuku, Japan's center of street fashion, or lolling about in Yoyogi Park, dressed up as a gothic character from that vein of anime and manga titles, or in a coy manga-inspired maid's outfit.

But costumed Americans are gathering together in the thousands almost weekly at anime conventions that, as Solomon says, now take place "all across America," to display their anime affection publicly. And the range of costumes on display, from *Akira*-inspired, spiky-haired boyishness to *Sailor Moon* schoolgirls and rocket-firing *Evangelion* robots, is nearly as striking as the diversity of participants.

"I found this year's Expo packed," Solomon says of the annual 2006 event, which is North America's largest and most prestigious. "And there were far more costumes than previously. At one point, I saw five guys dressed as Vash posing for a picture. But what I suspect is most significant is that over the years I've been attending, the sex ratio has shifted from a vast majority of males to a pretty even balance. It's also a very mixed crowd ethically—white, Asian, black, Latino."

Dr. Lawrence Eng, resident otaku expert at Rensselaer Polytechnic Institute (RPI), in Troy, New York, began attending Anime Expo and other conventions over a decade ago. "Back then, I saw a lot of people like myself—meaning, college-aged Asian males. But nowadays at anime cons, the demographic has clearly shifted. It could very well be about 50 percent females who now attend, with all different ethnicities represented, something closer to the normal U.S. ethnic distribution."

As a public manifestation of Japanamerica in the twenty-first century, the sudden proliferation of anime and manga conventions and expos in the United States that draw massive crowds of diverse races and sexes can hardly be beat. The first Anaheim expo (now called AX) was held fifteen years ago. Today, its Web site advises parents how to take care of their children "12 and under."

The shift, Eng notes, has been very recent. Today he finds "many more younger fans than before," from high school students on down. "College-aged fans still attend," he adds, "and some of us who were in college in the mid-'90's can still be found. But [our] numbers have dwindled in comparison."

Shunsuke Narutani, who works in Akihibara and is an authority on all things underground in Japan, takes me to a popular *Kos-Kyaba* (cosplay club) in Kanda, tucked into an alleyway blocks away from his office. Narutani defines Kos-Kyaba more expansively as a "costume-play casual cabaret club."

Outside the building is the club's logo on a lighted sign: a cartoon graphic of a starry sky and half moon above several crookedly angled and pointy-roofed buildings, the urban village below, lit from within. It is called Magical Night.

We rise in a dingy elevator to the fourth floor, where a bow-tied young male greets us at the door, takes our coats and shoulder bags, and politely tells us we have two hours to stay, before ushering us to our table.

The club is small, bathed in an aqua-blue light. Four small disco balls hang from the ceiling, spinning and glimmering.

The tables along the wall and in the center of the room feature purple Naugahyde upholstered banquettes and chairs. As soon as we are seated, two young women, one in a classic schoolgirl uniform, the other in a blue blouse, short skirt, and massive platform boots, and bearing a fuzzy-eared headband, take their seats close beside us.

In many respects, this is the classic setup for a Japanese hostess bar, in which pretty young women dressed either elegantly or suggestively, depending on the venue and the neighborhood, sit close to their male patrons throughout the evening, pouring drinks, lighting cigarettes, and flattering their clients with flirtatious repartee before being circulated to the next table by a hyperattentive male staff. Hostess clubs do not feature actual sex, but many of them do implicitly encourage after-hours liaisons, to keep the male clients coming back and bestowing upon the club, and the women themselves, wads of money and often lavish gifts.

The cosplay women also pour drinks, but the drinks are nonalcoholic or barely alcoholic, only a few containing light spirits that have only the mildest effects, and the drinks bear names lifted from popular manga, like Crescent Moon Margarita (with no tequila) or Fruits Basket Fruit Punch. They hand out fresh *oshibori*—moistened Japanese hand towels in restaurants and bars, delivered hot or cold, depending on the season. The women also light cigarettes for smokers and serve snacks. They grin expectantly and photogenically when you look at them. In my case, they ask me questions about America and New York, my work, what I like to do, and so on. Flirtatious questions, perhaps, but never overtly sexual, and since their costumes are far more interesting than anything I could possibly say, the conversation swiftly switches course: I am the one asking questions.

Like American expo-goers, they make their own costumes—and the club's management does not tell them who or what they must be. It is up to them alone to choose the character they wish to portray, and they clearly take well-deserved pride in what they produce. When I ask them why they chose their characters, the answers often come after deeply considered pauses. "She's cool and strong and weak, too," is a common theme. Or, as one decidedly midsize girl gleefully says: "She's fat, just like me!"

Finally, there is a pause in my conversation. When I take stock of the room, walking around en route to the lavatory, listening and watching, I notice that most of the men—in their early twenties to mid-forties—are engaged in serious conversations with their cosplay servers, discussing the motivations of a character in a given manga or anime episode and how the meanings might apply to their own lives. The men sit forward in their chairs or booths, brows furrowed, nodding. There are a few grins and giggles, but otherwise very little of what might be construed as giddy flirtation, and no expressions of overt or threatening sexuality, despite the erotic undertones. These are, after all, attractive women in their twenties wearing sometimes revealing costumes.

On the TV screen, an installment of *Ultraman Taro*—a Japanese series from the 1960s and 1970s, featuring a giant red-and-silver superhero alien with at least a half-human soul—suddenly appears in blazing color. Created by Eiji Tsuburaya, whose special-effects work helped produce Godzilla, Ultraman was one of my childhood heroes when I lived for part of a year with my grandparents in northern Japan. His insectlike eyes and horned silver head were no doubt part of what attracted me. And that he had limited power—signaled by the orb at the center of his chest that began to blink when his energies were fading—literally highlighted his mortality, his human side.

But watching the program now, I am reminded of Canadian Thomas Lee's comment about the directly confrontational nature of battle in the anime he loved as a child. Ultraman is, as always, fighting a mutant space monster, and this one looks like a mix between a giant shrimp and a spiny-backed beetle, an accident of irradiation. But Ultraman is not merely zapping the thing with lasers—or with a powerful web of entrapment, the way Spiderman would. He is engaging his adversary hand to hand, tossing the creature into buildings, fending off and sometimes absorbing powerful blows to his own body. It creates the sort of riveting spectacle of physical combat that some associate with professional wrestling, minus the egos, pointless acrobatic displays, and mindless storylines. Ultraman is saving the world from destruction. We need him.

A tuxedoed older man peers out at me from behind a door on the far side of the room and smiles. One of the cosplay staff, a woman in a tight silver suit with stars painted around her breasts, rushes to our table to explain. Narutani told the club's manager that I liked *Ultraman Taro*. He located this old episode in his DVD collection and is playing it for me.

Ultraman was also, I realize, my first encounter with cosplay. My mother took me to Tokyo Tower many years ago to meet him. Back then, when the skinny, very human-size costumed character reached out to take my hand, I was terrified.

But here I am lightheaded with pleasure. A dizziness similar to the one that bathed me in light at the Tokyo Anime Fair overtakes me. Costumed characters flit from table to table around me, fantasies come to life. Everyone in the room seems more serious about their dreams than their jobs. I have a fresh *oshibori* at hand, its hot steam rising against the chill winter night outside. I feel high—and I am drinking a grapefruit-flavored soda with no alcohol.

Afterward Narutani and I walk through the rain to the adjacent train station. I tell him cosplay is catching on in America, but he only shakes his head.

"Not like this, right?" he says, gesturing back toward the alleyway and Magical Night.

No, I tell him. Not quite like this.

On the train back to my apartment, I mull over an observation: In certain contexts, Japanese culture can combine the auras of sexual energy (the cosplay girls) and violence (Ultraman) without creating an atmosphere of seedy perversity or provocation. From what I could see, there was no lascivious leering on behalf of the customers, nor did I sense the unspoken threat of machismo on behalf of the club's management, despite the venue being discreet and clearly for adults only. There was no pressure to buy more drinks, and tipping is not accepted in Japan.

The focus was squarely on the costumes, the young women who made them, and the manga pages and anime scripts from which they sprang. This was a club for otaku.

Far deeper than the borrowed term "cosplay" is the very Japanese word we have also appropriated: "otaku." In the word's broader usage today, Narutani might be described as an otaku, given his encyclopedic knowledge of Japan's demimonde. I could be an otaku for my helpless infatuation with certain books, certain musical genres and bands, or Japanese and American cultures. The word can be used for anyone who is obsessed. Look in the mirror: You might be otaku, too.

More specifically, the word "otaku" defines an individual obsessed with manga and anime. A collector of the books, video-cassettes, DVDs, cards, toys, figurines, and so on, whose interest ranges well beyond the casual. It is another Japanamerican word that has undergone a dramatic evolution, both before and after it whizzed back and forth across the Pacific.

otakudom

Forty-one-year-old Hideki Ono does not appear happy. We are sitting in a third-floor café in Shinjuku on a rainy night. He looks sodden: a bit pudgy, tired, unshaven—someone who gets too little sleep and/or sunshine. His assistant, a pert twenty-two-year-old woman, rubs his shoulders and bucks him up when I enter the café, whispering "*ganbare*"—or "fight hard."

At first, Ono strikes me as a classic otaku, a dedicated and obsessive fan of anime and manga since early childhood, with a thorough knowledge of their histories, titles, and backgrounds. In college, he worked for *Animage* magazine, one of the biggest and longest-running publications in the industry. But when I suggest that he might be an otaku, he bristles a bit.

"I'm not one of the core otaku," he says. "They are more pure at heart. The articles I write are for them, the core audience. A lot of readers probably think of me as being a bit outside the mainstream."

Hideki Ono is not his real name. He asked me not to use his name, partly because of his position in the industry: He is the editor of an online Japanese anime magazine called *Anime Style*, which he founded as a print publication in 2000. He writes many of the articles himself, mostly critical analyses of anime aesthetics, essays, and reviews. Other columns and contributions are penned by anime artists, and Ono claims that the site receives 20,000 unique hits per day from what he calls "maniacs," anime fans who go beyond otaku extremes of passion and reach sublime immersion.

The term "otaku" has been embraced by Americans, I tell him, and there are fewer negative connotations in the American usage. Over the past two decades, people who used to be called geeks or nerds achieved a level of respect in America, largely via the success of the computer and its related industries. Bill Gates became a capitalist hero; craigslist is international.

I suspect this also had something to do with the shifting stereotype of the Asian male in America, who was often portrayed as a weak and geeky character associated with science, math, and computers. When the Internet millionaires began flashing signs of their success in the 1990s, Asian males, like Yahoo cofounder Jerry Yang, were prominent among them. As Cyndi Lauper once screeched, money changes everything, especially in America.

Though, as Dr. Eng notes, "there are still plenty of negative stereotypes surrounding anime," the use of the term "otaku" in the U.S. media is often lighthearted, an expression of pleasure, as in the headline of a recent issue of the *Boston Phoenix*, a weekly similar to New York's *Village Voice*. The paper's guide to the best anime, published prior to Boston's own three-day anime convention, was titled "Otaku You." And in spring 2006, Central Park Media, one of America's oldest Asian anime and film distributors, released a film made two years earlier titled *Otaku Unite!*

I ask Ono if he thinks the American usage of "otaku" has helped produce more positive connotations in Japan. His response is startling.

"There seem to be many otaku in America these days, but we actually learned it from you. America is where otaku started. When I was in junior high, Star Trek fans were the original otaku. They had activities and the costumes. Back then, America was already doing it. I never thought it would spread in Japan, too."

Devoted American fans of the *Star Trek* television series emerged in the 1960s wearing the costumes of their favorite characters and attending conventions. Ono's contention that they played a major role in inspiring otaku behavior is reminiscent of Tezuka, the father of anime, illustrating and publishing his own Bambi books in the 1950s.

"About ten years ago, a woman researcher from America interviewed me. She asked: 'Why do Japanese people act like otaku? Isn't it weird?' And I said, '*We* learned it from *you*.'"

In just the past two decades, "otaku" has gone from its original meanings in Japanese of a formal second-person address and an honorific term for another person's household—to its contemporary reference to a person who is densely obsessed. Along the way, it has also gone through some dark days in Japanese public opinion.

"When I was young," Ono says, "there was another word, *mi-ha*. It kind of means 'star struck.' About ten years ago, the *mi-ha* were fans of the cuter characters in manga. It was used even before anime appeared, to refer to someone who was kind of frivolous, and who pursued the popular. Then there were collectors, the *mania* folks. There was the standard anime fan, the *mi-ha* anime fan, and then the *mania*—the collectors."

This latter group, the collectors, is the meaning more pertinent to Americans today, though we do not call them "mania," and like most borrowed words in any culture, the term "otaku" as it is used in English is in many ways an American invention. The Japanese still have complicated responses to its nuances, whereas we have adopted it more aggressively, with broader applications of its meaning.

"Eventually, the *mi-ha* group became mainstream fans, the core audience," Ono says. "So I guess that's what's called 'otaku' in Japan now: the fans who are addicted to their favorite characters. And from that emerged cosplay, and probably the more sexual orientation of broader anime fandom."

Ono sips his coffee, grunting softly, and accepting another massage from his twenty-two-year-old charge.

The oft-repeated story of the origins of the word "otaku" goes like this: In the late 1970s and early 1980s, when anime and manga fans in Japan were first meeting one another at domestic conventions, they began to recognize one another's faces, though they did not know each other by name. By way of greeting, they said, "o-taku," roughly meaning "hey, you," though with the more formal, less casual intimations of the French second-person address, "vous." In American English, it might be more like, "Hello there, sir."

In 1983, when Japan's economy was well into its monumental rise, journalist Akio Nakamori wrote a serialized magazine story, "The Investigation of Otaku," explaining the term to common readers. Japan's manga/anime-obsessed nerds and geeks, he wrote, address one another by the following term: "O-taku."

After that, two news events helped redetermine the meaning of "otaku" in Japan.

In 1989, a serial child killer, Tsutomi Miyazaki, was arrested in Sendai, north of Tokyo, for the abduction, mutilation, and murder of four young girls. He was a loner with deformed hands whose apartment was filled with anime, some of which was violent and pornographic.

The Japanese media branded Miyazaki "the otaku murderer," and people who had never before heard of the term "otaku" came to know its pejorative meaning very well. The nation effectively shook its head in disapproval.

"['Otaku'] became a brand when Nakamori wrote about it," says Ono. "Then, when the killer was caught, it became a nationwide obsession."

But, he adds, the word was never entirely reduced by the oversimplifications applied to it. "Even [after the murders], 'otakus' were still perceived somewhat differently. They knew a ton about a certain subject, or they had a massive collection of one thing or another, or they had a lot of skills in one area. That was the nuance. There was even a Japanese movie in the 1980s called *The Seven Otaku*. It's about ugly men who have amazing capabilities, and terrific skills."

Having a hobby or two is a big deal in Japan. In a culture where remaining in office well after the dinner hour is still common practice—as is socializing with your boss and colleagues when you finally do leave—the deep investment that many Japanese make in their extracurricular activities may be seen as a necessary escape valve: the only way to truly get away from your job. Ono's comments remind me of what novelist Murakami said back in 2000, the first time I met him in his Tokyo writing studio. I asked him if he could explain the appeal of his books to younger readers.

"My protagonists are so lonely," he said, "but at least they have their styles, their obsessions to survive on. That means a lot. They don't know what the purpose of life is or what their goals are, but they have to live on in any case. It's kind of a stoic life, to survive strictly on your obsessions. It's also kind of religious, sometimes. You could say that it's a kind of postmodernist view— to survive a meaningless life strictly on your tastes in things, your styles. Sometimes my readers are impressed by that kind of stoicism."

Then he leaned back and sighed. "It's not easy, you know."

the otaku boom

If "otaku" are now cast in a more positive light on both sides of the Pacific, referring to an obsessive collector and a dead-serious hobbyist, it is partly because of the term's acceptance and use internationally—and partly because of an anime and manga best seller, released in Japan in 2005.

Called *Densha Otoko* (*Train Man*), the story first surfaced as a supposedly real account of a single evening. It appeared in a posting to Japan's (and the world's) biggest bulletin board Web site, "2ch," or 2 channel.

The narrator, a self-professed otaku, wrote of his chance encounter on one of Tokyo's many lengthy commuter rail rides. Sitting in a crowded car, he saw an older man groping a younger woman—one of the few crimes that is common in Japan, a type of sexual harassment or assault that is very culture specific. The women being violated frequently refuse to say a word out of embarrassment, and also, probably, out of the respect for others' privacy, a result of Japan's long history of living in small spaces.

No one else in the car reacted. But the otaku did, fending off the older man and drawing attention to his violations, thereby helping the young woman retain her dignity. A railway conductor finally intervened.

The woman thanked the otaku, exchanging business cards and addresses with him before she left the train. Days later, the otaku—the "train man"—received a pricy Hermes tea set as a gift of thanks from the woman.

Thereafter, the two began dating. They allegedly are still together now.

Whatever the truth of the story, it became a national and commercial sensation—culminating in several best-selling manga, a TV series, a feature film (currently being remade in the United States), and anime productions. *Train Man* resurrected the otaku image, just as Bill Gates and the Internet boom of the '90s may have helped elevate the image of American nerds.

Today, many young Americans speak proudly of their status: "We're otaku!" crowed some kids I met while visiting a Massachusetts junior high school's expanding anime club. While back in Japan, newspaper romance columnists weigh in on the merits and drawbacks of the otaku craze—whether the uber-obsessed might make good mates because they're devoted by nature, or whether the abstract objects of their devotions make them perpetually distracted, incapable of focusing on another human being. A recent article on the subject appeared in *Shukan*

Bunshun, a major Japanese magazine, and was cited by the *Mainichi Daily News*, one of Japan's three biggest dailies. Manga artist Mimei Sakamoto is quoted bemoaning the mainstreaming of otaku—the "otaku boom"—complaining that there are now too many people walking the streets of Japan sporting nerdy glasses. "Real otaku should go back and shut [them] yourselves off from the world again," the paper quotes her as saying. "The true value of being a real otaku lay in the belief that nobody else understands you."

"[Otaku] are now just people who live for their hobbies or interests," says Ono. "Compared to ten years ago, the word is no longer as discriminatory. And in just twenty years, the entire range of its meaning has broadened."

otaku by numbers

The otaku phenomenon has entered Japan's public consciousness as a way to explain the behavior not just of introverted teens, but also of millions of Japanese who supposedly put their life's interest on a pedestal—above their interest in their real lives.

But the mainstreaming of the word means that the lives of otaku are no longer curios. The behavioral oddities of otaku were once seen as petri dish samples for analysis, but otaku communities in Japan are now big and vibrant enough to dictate the way major supermarket goods and more conventional products are marketed, in addition to the way prime-time television programming is pitched. Otaku blogs have been published to become best sellers; districts of some major cities are being refurbished to cater to otaku shopping and leisure tastes.

The size of the self-declared otaku community in Japan has recently become a feature of serious financial analysis and intense media interest. In August 2005, Japan's biggest dailies solemnly covered the first-ever otaku Olympics—an event that attracted over half a million entrants.

Most of the otaku hopefuls were rejected from the competition during its first stage, which featured a twenty-page examination in which one hundred arcane questions taxed the true extent of the candidates' nerd quotients.

For example: If they did not know exactly how many more people attended the 2002 Tokyo *Comiket* (Comics Market) fan-made manga convention than the 2001 version, they did not make the cut. As one of the organizers of the exam told Leo Lewis of *The Times:* "Our aim is to nurture an otaku elite to carry the otaku culture through the twenty-first century."

According to a paper on the subject by the Nomura Research Institute, Japan's three million otaku now command a huge market. More than one million comic-book otaku spend more than a billion dollars every year buying comics and traveling hundreds of miles to conventions. An estimated eight hundred thousand "idol otaku"—those who are obsessed with Japan's plethora of pretty young pop singers—worship the individual stars and fritter away approximately six hundred million dollars on attending every single event in which the stars are involved. Around fifty thousand otaku devote their lives to the construction of computers from separate parts.

What the Nomura paper calls Japan's "enthusiastic consumers" now command a market worth around three billion dollars a year, without even including otaku interests that have now become accepted parts of the mainstream, such as the multibillion-dollar video game market.

When Lewis interviewed the report's compiler, Ken Kitabayashi, for *The Times*, the economist described otaku as "somewhat bizarre individuals," but conceded that the real market they represent is many times greater than what has been accounted for so far. "We are already working on a revised estimate that includes many other areas of otaku interest we didn't bring into the initial calculations. If you add in areas such as toy trains, real-train spotting, and the new breed of mobile phone otaku, the figure will be vast."

If Ono's analysis is accurate, the Trekkies may have created a monster in otaku.

But it is difficult to imagine the otaku scene in America growing quite as large or as intense as its counterpart in Japan. What the author Frederik Schodt, when discussing the nation's embrace of manga reading, described to me as Japan's "far more autistic, cramped, pressurized, and inward-looking lives" may be at least partly accountable for the drive to pursue an obsession to its outer limits.

diy

American otaku have grown increasingly aware of various otaku subgroups—such as *moe*, *yaoi/bishonen*, and *shojo* subcultures, and the *doujinshi*, comics made by the otaku themselves—that, like cosplay, move the action from the page or screen and into the participatory.

Moe is the most recent trend in the bunch. Ono tells me that *moe* otaku "feel an intense desire" and "deep romantic longing" for the object(s) of their affections—in this case, extremely cute, beautifully drawn, and usually quite young-looking girls. But their distance from the object, and the absence of consummation of any kind, is as critical as their desire is powerful.

"The feeling has nothing to do with overt sexuality," Ono insists. *Moe* otaku feel "no desire to ask the subject out on a date, or ask her to marry you, or sexually harass her. It's just: Keep your distance while your feelings and emotions for her rise and increase."

But surely somewhere in that deep romantic longing lies a sexual charge?

Ono pauses. "There is an erotic nature inside the emotion," he admits. "But the person will never take the next step of action of any sort."

His defensive posture is understandable: *Moe* is one of the most controversial otaku subcultures in both Japan and the United States. The prevalence of images of underage girls, occasionally, though not commonly, involved in overtly sexual activities, has caused anime and manga fans, artists, and critics to debate its propriety. In a poll conducted in 2005 by the Anime News Network, an online portal for anime information, 29 percent of American anime fans felt that *moe* images should be banned completely. And in Sakamoto's rant, reported in the *Mainichi Daily News*, she accused *moe* otaku of having a "pedophiliac fetish."

Dr. Eng describes himself as a fan of *moe*-style graphics. "I like the artwork of *moe* anime in general," he says. "They're designed to be visually appealing, after all, [though] I don't find myself very excited by anime stories that heavily feature characters intended to be *moe*."

Eng elaborates on the *moe* controversy in his blog: "It is true that some anime and game characters designed to be attractive to otaku are very young looking (clearly drawn to look like minors, in other words), a fact that has certain moral implications to be worked out by the individual who chooses whether or not to like them. So far, in the United States, even when such drawings are explicitly pornographic (and most of them are not), they have been deemed legal and protected speech, in that they do not directly harm real-life children (unlike actual child pornography, which is widely agreed to be a form of child exploitation and abuse)."

In Japan, the popularity of the *moe* otaku trend has not resulted in an increase in crimes against children, sexual or otherwise. Instead, the effect has been more benign, but definitely pronounced. Maid cafés, in which the objects of *moe* otaku affections serve coffee and tea in their frilly short-skirted costumes, have been cropping up on Tokyo street corners with a frequency equal to that of Japanese restaurants appearing in Manhattan. Ono calls it "the maid boom," and deconstructs its central appeal. "The maid calls you 'master' only because she is a maid. There's no personal reason. But you feel like you are needed."

The maids speak in the squeaky high-pitched singsong tones that define feminine *kawaii* (cuteness) in Japan. They are submissive, looking up to you as though you were someone respectable (a master!), reliable, and, to some extent, protective.

"The tension between the distance and the longing is what's critical," adds Ono.

But won't that tension, carried to extremes, eventually become frustrating?

Finally, Ono smiles. "When that happens," he says, "the *moe* otaku has an option: He can buy the figurines."

Yaoi otaku are women who consume manga and anime featuring love stories between beautiful boys—the *bishonen*.

Yaoi has a longer history than *moe*. Ono claims that the female otaku subculture "has been around forever," but says that it began to surface as a notable audience two decades ago. And while the male characters portrayed are definitely romantic, and sometimes are sexual at the pornographic end of the spectrum, they are not, strictly speaking, portrayed as homosexuals. "It's not exactly gay— it's more of an organically occurring romantic love without having the self-consciousness of gayness. It could just be friendship, or it could be lovemaking."

Where the male *moe* otaku have their maid cafés in Akihabara, the *yaoi* women have their own "boy's love district" in the Ikebukuro neighborhood in northwest Tokyo. Smaller in size than Akihabara, the area is nonetheless rife with bookshops selling boy's love manga and fan-made manga, featuring huge billboards and posters showing embracing men often on the verge of a kiss. And, of course, there are boy's love cafés, the *yaoi* counterpart to maid cafés, but there's a hitch: They are staffed by beautiful young women dressed up like men, in all likelihood because it is impossible to find men who can approximate the ideal looks and grace- fulness of the *bishonen*—or at least impossible to find enough of them to staff a café.

As has been noted elsewhere, there are manga covering every subject imaginable in Japan. But the clear dividing lines between the sexes of their consumers, and the distinct ways in which they are targeted, can be seen as yet another example of Japan's innate knack for postmodernity. Only in the past decade or so have Americans begun speaking of "chick flicks" and "chick lit," of a mass audience that has fractured into narrower and more focused consumer segments, causing CD and DVD stores to split their inventory stock into numerous niches. With manga and anime, the Japanese adjusted to this reality years ago.

But the *yaoi* audience, which Ono says is much larger than the *moe* crowd, is particularly relevant to manga importers to the United States. Conventionally, cartoons and comic books in America were not only for kids; they were largely thought to be for boys only. But as the *New York Times* reported in 2004, one of the central driving forces behind the spike in U.S. manga sales was manga's popularity among girls.

Shojo manga, targeting young female readers, have a long history in Japan, and the audience raised on them makes up the *yaoi* subculture. In a process that TokyoPop CEO Levy calls "aging up" the readership, the manga audience in Japan has had generations in which to develop its tastes, with its female readers advancing from *shojo* titles about adventurous and thoughtful girls to *bishonen* love or erotic stories between romantic and gorgeous men.

"What happened is that manga grew as a market in Japan starting with kids in the 1950s," Levy says. "Then, generation by generation, from those kids onward, manga kept being read. Those kids are now in *their* 50s, and they now read classic mangas."

Naturally, Levy hopes to replicate this process in the United States. "But in America, this is just the first manga generation. In the first few years of our company, they encountered *Sailor Moon*," the title that TokyoPop exported to the United States in the late 1990s, to great success. "But now [those kids] are twelve, thirteen, fourteen, and fifteen years old. And they are becoming the big fans of *shojo* or fruits manga."

Levy is confident that he can build a cross-generational, cross-gender audience that is as manga savvy as the one in Japan, though he acknowledges that it will take some time. "It will age up," he says. "But there's a lot of Japanese titles we can't try to import now because it has not had time to happen yet. Those great manga created for Japanese eight-year-olds back in the 1960s and 70s—there's just no market for them in the U.S." A look of disappointment crosses his face as he shakes his head. "The older generation in the U.S., they're still into Spider Man and stuff."

The appeal of *shojo* manga to American girls (which "made it our biggest growth sector" in the early twenty-first century, notes Levy) is often explained by references to manga's superior story lines and psychological complexities. But the *Times* article also points to the more modest physical proportions of many female *shojo* manga characters, enhancing their believability for young female readers—and perhaps making them seem less intimidating.

"*Sailor Moon*, for example, is very different from *Charlie's Angels*," says Ono, explaining the aesthetics of Japanese female heroines. "She's not really masculine—she's small and fragile. But she's powerful. That's very Japanese."

Also very Japanese, he believes, is the emphasis on female and child characters, not just in *shojo* titles, but in all manga and anime. He theorizes that Asians in general, and Japanese especially, like to have more diminutive characters performing heroic feats—David beating Goliath—partly because they are physically smaller than most other ethnicities. It is a theory that dovetails nicely with Japan's general, centuries-old self-image: the little island—battered by storms, invading foreigners, and, more recently, nuclear bombs—that could.

"There's always an emphasis on women and children, maybe because a lot of Asians feel smaller and more fragile than other races," Ono says. "Especially in Japan, we love seeing women and children." He reels off a list of Japanese fairy tales, including Tezuka's anime *Astro Boy*, featuring children as heroes: resourceful, clever, but also strong.

"It's about little kids beating the bad guys, who are adults," he says. "For example, Amuro, the hero of *Mobile Suit Gundam*, is fifteen years old. If the Americans made it, he wouldn't be that young."

Aside from possibly growing weary of more clichéd notions of the heroic, younger Americans are also maturing in a world of rising interactivity, from the Internet to video games. It may well be more satisfying for them to read manga or watch anime with heroic characters who are less like role models than direct models, less like who they might or are supposed to become, more like themselves. Online, kids can interact in real time with friends; can post or download their own homemade videos, songs, or anime; can enter chat rooms, narrate blogs, and create their own Web sites—and identities. In many video games, they can choose characters, settings, levels of play, soundtrack music, and more, and they are active in making choices that literally create several of the game's narrative elements.

"I think Japanese people tend to like seeing women and children as active heroes," Ono concludes. "I don't know why, exactly, but it's just more fun to see. Maybe Americans are beginning to feel that way, too."

doujinshi

Tellingly, the first examples of *doujinshi* are probably the Disney-based *Bambi* and *Snow White* books published by Osamu Tezuka, the very father of anime, in the 1950s. An uber-fan of the American master, Tezuka was also an ardent consumer of the master's products, paying admission to the "eighty" movie showings he claims to have seen—so that he could reproduce them accurately.

Japan's domestic *doujinshi* subindustry is nearly as large as the original manga publishing industry itself. Japan's otaku churn out pages drawn in the style, and featuring the characters, of their favorite titles, publish them, and sell them—all without being prosecuted for breaching copyright laws, and all in the name of interactive fun.

Doujinshi reproductions, mimics, and homages to professional manga and anime artists have been a part of the communal business for two decades or more, says Narutani as he guides me through a four-story *doujinshi* shop nestled in the alleyways of Akihabara's east side. But they are not all as respectable as Tezuka's Disney books. Some feature mainstream characters in pornographic scenarios. Others mix and match characters from various anime titles, and show them in violent disarray.

Who makes the money? I ask Narutani.

He shrugs. "I guess the otaku do," he says. "Or just the stores selling their stuff."

In fact, as one manga editor would later tell me, some *doujinshi* have made so much money that they fear the tax man, who might wonder how they purchased their split-level condominiums and vintage Corvettes, far more than they do copyright lawyers.

Doujinshi are evidence of a radically different approach to copyright boundaries from what we are accustomed to in the United States. But they are also a signifier of Japan's appreciation for a democracy of aesthetics. Debates swirl annually about the Japanese approach to education, the rote-learning techniques that tend to crowd out creativity and individualism. But as the British journalist Lewis reminds me: The techniques do teach kids how to draw, or play the piano, or solve math and science problems.

"For research on a story about Japanese education, I visited a Japanese school last year on a warm sunny day," he says. "There was a recess break when I arrived. I expected the kids to be out on the playground, kicking soccer balls about. But they were all inside—drawing. In fact, they were mostly quiet, concentrating, but one kid looked up and asked his classmate: 'How do you do the hair?' "

Eyeing the vast array of *doujinshi* reproductions, I am overwhelmed by the scenarios: recognizable characters from Gundam featured in perverse yet fantastically eye-catching situations. All of it for sale, and all of it, apparently, unmonitored.

Here is an attempt at an American parallel: Imagine a series of novels featuring Holden and Phoebe Caulfield—in outer space, or engaging in incestuous activities—and the creator(s) of the series being either ignored by the litigators of J.D. Salinger's estate, or possibly flattered by them.

For help and sanity, I ask TokyoPop's Levy about what's going on, and why it is allowed and encouraged.

"Look," he begins, leaning forward with palms open, as if counseling a new student. "The *doujinshi* make porn and parody. So they'll show *Initial D*, for example, where Takumi's getting a blowjob while he's driving."

Is that legal?

"No, it's totally illegal to publish these things, but it's tolerated. In Japanese, there's a phrase—*anmoku-no-ryoukai*—that roughly means 'permission of the dark,' which is the most literal translation, a kind of tacit approval. The publishers are all aware, but they just look the other way. The artists either look the other way, or they're just pleased by the attention."

Cultural sayings and proverbs are revealing, of course, and one that grants permission for "dark" activities reminds me of another, one that I learned from a Japanese college student: *Akashingo, minna de watareba kowaku-nai*, or "Red lights—if everyone crosses against them together, there's nothing to be afraid of."

A like-minded community of fans, artists, and publishers producing and reproducing one another's artwork, crossing together against the red lights of copyright infringement, can afford to be fearless. At least in Japan.

I ask Levy what he, as an importer of manga into the United States, a publisher and producer with offices in both countries, thinks about the absence of copyright enforcement.

"With *Princess Ai*," he says, referring to one of his company's biggest international book projects, allying the American rock star Courtney Love with a Japanese manga artist, "if there's fan fiction on the Web or a fan manga floating around, I'd be really pleased. I'd feel honored. It's flattering. But maybe if Ai were being raped by the male characters in the story, I'd be pretty pissed off." He pauses, rubbing his fashionable three-day-old whiskers. "At the same time, I might feel, wow, I'd made it all the way to porn! And I'd definitely want a copy."

In some respects, *doujinshi* represent an obvious future for content producers worldwide. As more and more content becomes accessible, and as interactivity becomes the norm—with blogs and Web sites like YouTube.com that enable users to post their own videos for the world to see, many of which are creative pastiches of other originals (the way sampling functions in hip-hop)—the question of originality becomes moot, quaintly old school. Maybe someone else created Holden Caulfield, but what if you could place him in an episode of *The O.C.*, or *Sex and the City*, just to see how he fares?

In others, the *doujinshi* creations are admirably democratic. While the shops are filled floor to ceiling with fan-produced products, you are not obliged to buy any of them, and there is no pretense to originality. Anyone can create a *doujinshi* rip-off. In just one shop, passing through the narrow aisles between shelves stacked several high, the choices and variations seem virtually endless. They sell only if they are good—if they have earned a reputation with those in the know, or are especially appealing to passersby.

Some *doujinshika* (fan-artists) earn more than a reputation: They get careers, acquire an audience, and rise to the level of professionals themselves. Two teams of professional manga artists, CLAMP and Gainax, both of which have amassed followings in the United States (CLAMP's manga is distributed by TokyoPop), began as *doujinshika*. And some professional manga artists, most notably Ken Akamatsu of *Love Hina*, create *doujinshi* titles under pseudonyms and sell them at the massive annual *doujinshi* Comiket (Comics Market) in Tokyo.

2dk's d'Heilly sees it as another example of a Mobius-strip-like exchange, this one between artist and audience. "In '95 you had *Evangelion*, where even the *doujinshi* were recognized by the director. You know, Hideaki Anno was throwing their stuff, their ideas and graphics, into his work, and winking back. He's saying, 'Here, guys!'"

Perhaps some are resistant because they still cling to the primacy of the artist as a sacred original. But that is a slower, monolithic, and more analog-hardened mentality. Maybe the rest of the world, as it did on and after 9/11, is taking off without people who think like that.

make and play: american doujinshi

"More and more [American] anime fans are learning about fan activities," says Dr. Eng. "Things such as cosplay, and creating their own artwork. Even if the American anime industry suddenly disappeared, the fan community would remain very strong."

But Americans catching on to fan-based art face two major obstacles: the difficulty of finding and financing cooperative printers, and the bright red lights of American copyright laws, not to mention their considerably more plentiful, more astringent, and more fearful legal enforcers.

Not insurmountable obstacles, perhaps, but also not insignificant. Self-publishing is on the rise in both countries, of course, and with advances in computer publishing software and technologies, it may well result in shadow subcultures of production and economy, especially as niche markets continue to subdivide into smaller, more narrowly focused readerships.

But in a nation as vast and rural as the United States is, distribution is one of the great banes of any American publisher, personal or professional. Schlepping the books from region to region, city to city, and town to town requires considerable financial resources, and the brand-name clout that will help the books get displayed in the first place.

In response, American otaku, like an increasing number of blog-making young American would-be writers, are using the Internet to spread the creative wealth.

"It's been my impression that American *doujinshi* writers tend to put their creations up on the Web rather than print them out as Japanese fans do," says *Super #1 Robot*'s Matt Alt, conceding that he, like others I spoke to, are wandering into new, relatively uncharted terrain. "A system for circulating physical copies does not really exist in the U.S.A. as it does in Japan. As with many other aspects of American otakudom, I suspect the majority of American *doujinshi* writers are reacting to what the Japanese are doing, rather than reflecting any kind of spontaneous outgrowth of American fan desires in and of themselves."

Alt may be right—at least for now.

TokyoPop's Stuart Levy and other American importers with one foot in both nations are fully aware of the interactive appeal of anime, manga, and their wealthy distant cousin, video games. Younger generations are weaned on interactivity. They are not content merely to watch and consume; they want to make and play.

A longtime American otaku guru who goes by the name of "John" hosts a portal for anime inquiry called Anime Nation. His response to a query about the rising numbers of American *doujinshi* is worth recording here:

"Westerners have, until very recently, always approached Japanese comics and animation as an established medium—something complete and finished, to be appreciated—not a work in progress or something to be embellished," he writes. "Fan fiction and *doujinshi* have never been common among English-speaking fans. Instead, English-speaking fans have tended to utilize and reconstruct existing anime through editing to create music videos. While Japanese natives create manga and anime, westerners just import, watch, collect, and manipulate manga and anime. We don't create Japanese art ourselves.

"But," he adds, "that stereotype is changing. American works like *MegaTokyo*, *Peach Fuzz*, and *Shadow Magic* can be thought of as extended *doujinshi*."

Peach Fuzz is one of TokyoPop's most popular titles. At the beginning of the century, CEO Levy began cultivating American *doujinshi* aggressively, through a campaign and contest called Rising Stars of Manga—a solicitation of manga submissions from its most ardent fans, via the Internet.

Peach Fuzz is the manga-inspired creation of two Americans, Lindsay Cibos and Jared Hodges of Florida, the *doujinshika* winners of TokyoPop's early "Rising Stars" competition. The story features a nine-year-old girl who must learn about maternal responsibility through her dearest friend: a pet ferret, given to the girl by her mother. The daughter must learn to care for and train her ferret friend; but the ferret, too, must learn not to regard its human companion's fingers as . . . monsters.

Peach Fuzz was the publisher's first title to go into syndication in a wide selection of America's Sunday newspapers, at the start of 2006—and there are increasing calls from fans demanding an anime version.

Sitting up with enthusiasm in his Tokyo office, Levy believes that his American *doujinshi* strategy has legs.

"We're up to the fifth contest," he says, reaching up to racks around the small room to exhibit paperback copies of titles by successful entrants. "The first one we did, we got over a thousand entries. Because there are lots of contests here in Japan, the number of entries is much lower. But we are one of the few in America, and the quality has risen dramatically. The American fans really are learning how to make manga. We call it the 'manga revolution,' " he adds, adeptly sliding into the conversation his company's tagline. "It's taking the Japanese spirit of manga and combining it with the local culture to get a multiethnic approach to the storytelling."

Quite a mouthful—and quite an electric charge. After a full day of touring Japan's major and midsize animation studios, visiting with articulate but decidedly reserved and sometimes solemn producers and artists, Levy has the pogo-stick enthusiasm of someone who spends half of his day on a trampoline.

"It's symbolic of the direction our company has to take," he says, with an eye firmly on the future of manga and anime in America. "We are moving from becoming 100 percent licensed, to a manga and book creator as well. We're not the only ones, but we're the most innovative."

Levy is most thrilled by the opportunity to cultivate a new generation of Japan-influenced manga and anime artists—not hailing from Japan, but from America, Europe, China, Korea, and elsewhere. And he thinks the time is right. America is undergoing a spike of interest in, and acceptance of, graphic storytelling as a sophisticated medium, he explains, with younger generations especially appreciative of the styles and aesthetics of Japanese graphic stories.

More important: American and foreign interest is rising just as Japanese interest in their indigenous graphic forms is dropping off.

"Let's face it: Japan is in a lull right now, in manga and in animation," Levy says. "What we're now trying to do in America is take what was wonderful about Japanese manga and anime and inspire another generation of writers overseas, who can then create new work influenced by both cultures. Then we can bring that inspiration back to Japan and hopefully inspire new work here."

It's a Japanamerican twist worthy of the British Invasion.

When today's British rock 'n' roll superstars, most of whom are now in their sixties and are still selling out U.S. stadiums, were teenagers, they were enamored with American blues and roots music. American musicians like John Lee Hooker struggled to fill nightclubs in American cities. But when they went to London, they played to sold-out concert halls, filled to the brim with ardent British youngsters like Pete Townshend, Mick Jagger, and John Lennon. Shortly thereafter, British bands brought their version of reculturized American blues to Americans—and became today's icons.

America's inability or unwillingness to appreciate its home-grown blues makers fifty years ago has echoes in the predicament expressed by manga and anime producers in the early years of Japan's twenty-first century, though the situation is less dire. Manga book sales, in particular, have dropped off dramatically—precipitously, by some domestic publisher's accounts—partly because readers young and old are now fully engaged by their high-tech, and more immediately gratifying, cell phones, video games, and Internet activities.

But others see a decline in the freedom and creativity of the Japanese industries themselves, like a band selling out, or those British rock icons becoming household names without producing anything innovative for decades.

Schodt is particularly scathing on this point, arguing that the new corporate shape of Japan's entertainment industry is killing off its inventiveness. "The days of experimentation, and the thrill of pioneering in new, exciting industries, are gone. Manga sales have dropped quite dramatically in Japan in the last ten years, and are now at 1996–1997 levels. Both the manga and anime industries are now mature businesses. Even the game industry has not been doing as well as some might think. Corporatization and standardization do not promote creativity. Creativity likes new, slightly disruptive environments."

The disruptions of World War II, the driving force behind the invention of the industry, according to Takashi Murakami, are long forgotten in Japan, despite the Asian antagonism toward Japanese prime ministers' visits to Yasukuni shrine, honoring the war dead and war criminals. Alt, in his early thirties, thinks this is partly responsible for Japan's dying interest in a weakening art form.

"That engine that drove the great manga and anime—the postwar sense of apocalypse—is gone. All artists can do now is ape the emotions of their predecessors. They don't have the same resonance. It's a good thing, really—I don't want them to experience the horror of a bombed-out Tokyo. But trauma creates art. If Japan had not had a nuclear bomb dropped on them, they probably wouldn't have made this beautiful art. I think Murakami's dead on. It's not even arguable. When you give a sexually abused kid crayons and a piece of paper, they'll start drawing sexual illustrations. Give him crayons, give him paper."

But we Americans have now experienced something akin to "the horror." A bomb-scarred New York. A fiery Pentagon. So can we now return to the Japanese the favor of their artistic trauma—the way the British reminded us of our race-based pain in the 1960s and beyond? 9/11 was our mushroom cloud, our ground zero. We have not fully recovered.

Of all the cultures that we know and acknowledge, only the Japanese culture has learned the same sense of mystical apocalypse, and it was learned from us.

"Put it this way," says Levy: "We've switched places. Disney and Pixar people today would be as thrilled to meet Miyazaki as Tezuka was to meet Disney in the 1960s."

8
future shocks

The timing of America's rising fascination with contemporary Japanese culture could hardly have been better. Childhood obsessions with Power Rangers, Dragon Ball, and Sailor Moon exploded into the Pokemon phenomenon. A Disney-powered distribution deal for Studio Ghibli brought Hayao Miyazaki's masterworks to the nation's multiplex screens, where the artist, like most serious film directors, believes his work should be seen. The founding of American- and Japan-based manga importers and publishers was met by a reading frenzy at chain bookstores and school libraries, where manga-focused discussion groups and after-school events have become as commonplace as anime conventions in American cities. DVDs ushered less family-oriented anime classics into American living rooms, where the mushroom clouds, mecha battles, and unflinching sexuality of philosophizing artists like Mamoru Oshii and Hideaki Anno illuminated the darker corners of our post-9/11 minds. Finally, all of this coincided with advances in broadband Internet technology, thrusting Japan's anime style into an immediate, pixel-sharp focus, and enabling new generations of American fans to graduate from TV series and collectible cards to hardcore anime otakudom—if Japan's artistic visions of apocalypse, adventure, romance, and liberated sexuality appealed to their maturing sensibilities.

"You basically had a generation of kids who went from Pokemon to Gundam Wing hentai in a single mouse click," says author Patrick Macias. "Anime and manga would have remained a much smaller phenomenon if Americans couldn't see what the Japanese model of fandom was supposed to look like. Cosplay, *doujinshi*, calling yourself an 'otaku'—this is all an imitation of what Americans perceive the model of Japanese fandom to be."

Before the Internet, he adds, "it was just about a bunch of people getting together in a room to watch stuff on TV."

Whether the generational boom in anime and manga will transform into a future fascination with Japanese culture is debatable, though there are some signs that it may already be happening. A recent story in the *Washington Post* notes that the number of Americans studying Japanese surged from 127,000 in 1997 to an estimated 3 million in 2006. According to Misako Ito of the

Japan Foundation—whose global offices promote the study of Japanese culture and language—the number of young Americans enrolling in Japanese language courses began to rise in the early years of this century. And unlike their predecessors, she says, the new students are not signing up to learn business Japanese. They want to converse more casually, and to be able one day to read and comprehend original editions of titles like *Sailor Moon* and *Naruto*.

The growing American passion for and access to Japanese pop is not a one-way street: It has also been driven by a near-simulta-neous rise in the quantity and the quality of Japan's contempo-rary creative output. Artists and designers like Takashi Murakami, Nigo, and DJ Krush; novelists like Banana Yoshimoto and Amy Yamada; and countless other Japanese hipsters began to flash on American media radars during the same time period. Hip-hop DJs started crisscrossing the Pacific to sample one another's styles.

Younger Japanese had grown up amid the wealth of the post-war Japan Inc. machine just as its cogs were starting to falter. But instead of stymieing them, the resulting slump actually cultivated their creativity. In a weak job market, graduates and dropouts alike had little to lose. And through the examples of their postwar par-ents and grandparents, as well as the rigors of an educational sys-tem in a nation with a 99 percent literacy rate, they already knew how to work hard.

"The recession was enormously productive for [Japan's] coun-terculture," says 2dk's David d'Heilly. "Previously these people were at Dentsu [the world's largest advertising agency] cranking out Honda ads. Now they're setting up their own indie fashion labels, or coding for the Web, or doing other things that are closer to what they want to be doing. The Japanese were always literate about all kinds of subcultures, and now they have a lot to add to them. They're great global ambassadors."

Novelist Haruki Murakami points to the role that adversity, albeit in a relatively mild form, played in fostering Japan's less cor-porate cultural identity: "When we were rich in the 1980s, we weren't producing any kind of international culture. But when we got poor again, we got humble. Then we became creative." For a writer who decades ago refused to join the ranks of his generation's blue-suited salarymen, and instead set out with a loan from his in-laws to manage a jazz club and write literature, Murakami's assessment is perhaps predictable, but it is also poignant. "It's still very hard to be an individual, very lonely," he says. "But ultimately, this is a good thing [for Japan]."

For Americans who were adolescents during Japan's bubble years, it would have been difficult to foresee the good thing that has resulted from the rise of Japanamerica. My own perceptions were partly shaped by teenage visits to Tokyo, where I caught a glimpse of the culture's color and felt its acquisitive energies. (I still recall entering a Shibuya record store and finding stacks of bootleg recordings of my favorite bands.) But no one else I knew was launching off to Tokyo then. American stereotypes of Japanese either saw them as rigidly bland and hyperserious, or were insulting—as in the bucktoothed tourist with glasses toting a camera. Based on these stereotypes, few Americans (besides businessmen keen to get in on the action) would have wanted to make the trip.

Author and manga historian Frederik Schodt believes that the time lag between its economic and cultural ascents may be working in Japan's favor today.

"American pop culture completely transformed Japanese comics and animation and music in the postwar period," he says. "But until recently, Japan was a bit of a pop-culture backwater. Not many Americans paid attention. This, conversely, allowed Japanese artists to develop what were otherwise very American forms of entertainment into something slightly different."

In Schodt's analysis, part of the explanation for the timing of Japanamerica is Americans' innate familiarity with certain borrowed elements in Japanese popular culture—the inevitable result of decades of cross-pollination.

"If you look at manga, anime, pop music," he says, "superficially they are extremely similar to what is available in America. But they are also a little different. The similarities make them understandable to Americans, and also nonthreatening, especially compared to highly inscrutable [traditional] art forms such as Noh. But the differences also make them very appealing."

Shizu Yuasa, d'Heilly's wife and 2dk business partner, grew up in Tokyo during Japan's pop-culture backwater years. Her memories corroborate Schodt's take on the slow accrual of American and other influences that led to the development of Japan's hybrid styles.

"I was around in the '70s and '80s, and all I listened to was foreign music, or I watched foreign movies. Nothing happening here was interesting to me. And in terms of fashion, we were awful in the '80s. The girls' fashion magazines just taught us to copy stuff: 'Street snap from Paris,' 'Street snap from New York.' But now, those same magazines are using 'Street snap from Tokyo' or 'Osaka.' "

As anthropologists have noted, Japan's is a culture of acquisition rather than of absorption. Japan is an island nation stuck in Shimizu's "in-between" world—with a major continent on either side, each with diverging views, practices, and beliefs. Japan acquires what it likes (or what will work) and localizes it, rejecting or gradually shrugging off what it does not like. So, tempura from the Portuguese, but not their chunky potatoes and onions.

Anime and manga artists, of course, were flourishing in those latter decades of the twentieth century. And although there are no direct parallels, since Japan was open as it never had been before, it is tempting here to think of the nation's isolationist streak, most pronounced during its two-hundred-plus years of the Tokugawa era. While Japan rose to global prominence in the 1970s and 1980s, a flourishing underground world of artists acquired what it liked from American, European, and Asian cultures and produced original work—but only for its own archipelago-bound audience, which shared a core cultural matrix of perceptions, visual icons, narrative assumptions, and fantasies. As in the Edo years, Japan was assiduously studying other cultures, but addressing its own creative expressions to the home-team crowd.

And today, as it was 150 years ago, it is largely the knock of the Americans on the front gates that is forcing Japan to pry those gates open. In 1854 it was Commodore Matthew Perry and his armada of "black ships"; today it is Hollywood and an armada of TV and DVD producers, distributors, publishers, and licensing contractors.

"To many young Americans, Japanese pop culture has a feeling of being 'fresh,' " says Schodt, "and it can therefore be perceived as an alternative to native [U.S.] pop-culture traditions that in some cases, such as comics and animation, and even music, feel quite ossified today."

The future seems bright for anime and manga, especially in America. The question is: Will it still be Japanese?

For American author and otaku Matt Alt, the answer is a definite no.

Alt is a nearly lifelong collector of Japanese-style model robots, many of which appear in manga and/or anime series. After graduating from college he followed his passion to Japan, where he settled in 1996, married a Japanese woman, and founded a translation company called AltJapan. He and his wife Hiroko work together on translation projects for video game and anime production companies, and Alt is sometimes called in as "a focus group of one" to assess a given title's chances overseas. "There's now a realization that the rest of the world is watching," he says.

Alt's proximity to the anime, manga, toy, and game industries (and his relentless enthusiasm for them) makes him an astute observer of their current conditions. He tells me that he recently went out for drinks with Shinji Aramaki, director of *Appleseed* and a professional robot maker, and was so nervous he was shaking.

We meet in a wood-paneled *izakaya* (Japanese-style tapas bar) on the Showa-dori side of Akihabara station, opposite the consumer electronics district that is otaku central in Tokyo, but close enough to feel its neon vibe. "I'm not antiglobalization, but the thing that really bothers me is this: When Japanese people get so worried about what the rest of the world thinks, they stop making what they love," he begins. "Self-consciousness destroys art. There's no way you can please everybody."

Alt's theory is that the anime medium peaked as long ago as the 1980s, when Japanese anime artists were more liberal, even punk-rock anarchistic in their approach to storytelling, serving their own needs before those of their audiences, at home or abroad. He cites 1986's *Fist of the North Star* as an example. "I loved the 'throw-everything-in' attitude of that TV series. Kids riding on motorcycles, beating the crap out of each other. Completely degenerate. It was as if the artists said—let's just make something cool."

Robotech, released the same year in the United States, was a watershed in the history of anime imports. Also produced by the Yoshida brothers of Tatsunoko Productions, makers of *Speed Racer* and *Battle of the Planets*, *Robotech* became the first major Japanese anime to be broadcast to American viewers largely intact, without the meddling of a Sandy Frank or the whitewashing of U.S. censors. And it became a major success, spawning an entire merchandizing franchise that included, of course, Alt's beloved robots.

"*RoboTech* was what knocked me out. I was in sixth grade. When my friends and I realized there was a theatrical release in Japan, we went crazy getting it. There was even a nude scene—it was so adult. And we were watching something like a tenth-generation dub. They were fighting in a snowstorm of static! But I remember thinking, wow, there's a place on this planet where people take this seriously."

Alt compares *Robotech* to Stanley Kubrick's *2001: A Space Odyssey*, calling it an apotheosis of its medium, made at a time when Japanese animators were unaware of an international audience and were striving for sophistication in their craft while still taking wild artistic risks. He says that the turning point toward self-consciousness is marked by Hideaki Anno's *Evangelion*, originally broadcast in Japan in 1995.

"A lot of people say that's the line after which the Japanese started taking anime more seriously. And then the international audience got into it, and the whole aesthetic changed. Things got more detailed, more elaborate, but not necessarily better. Anime had sort of reached the level of Hollywood film. Anime as its own discrete medium is dead, actually. There's not much difference to me anymore between *Innocence* and *The Matrix*. They're both beautiful films. That's it."

Even in the Internet era, there is always a perception lag between cultures whose time zones, languages, and sensitivities remain so distinct, and whose borders are so distant. This is particularly true if you do not happen to live in an urban center.

The possibility that Americans in greater numbers are discovering cool Japan just as its chief cultural export has hit a creative plateau cannot be good news for the artists, producers, and executives who are, in part, banking their future on increased international exposure.

It is not news at all to longtime fans like Schodt, who is from the first-generation wave of Japanamerican otakus, and who refers to historical precedent to support Alt's misgivings.

"Americans and others have a history of discovering and getting excited about dying Japanese art forms, without realizing they are dying," Schodt says. "It was true of ukiyo-e, and it was true with geisha and probably lots of other things, including 'Japanese management.' "

Schodt believes that the oppressive nature of the Japanese management structure itself—its notoriously hierarchical, obfuscated, and insular workings, as well as its conservative, consensus-seeking, and entropic tendencies—lies at the very heart of the anime/manga industry's terminal state. "The structure of the industry has sucked the life out of many manga, and also animated works," he says.

At the heart of that industry structure is Toei Animation. Founded in 1956 and meant to serve as a rival to Disney, Toei Animation is a giant in Japan, one of its oldest surviving anime and motion picture studios, and also one of its most old-fashioned.

"In the financial analysts' reports, at least, Toei is everything that you might want a Japanese anime company to be," says *Times* business journalist Leo Lewis. "Its products are popular nearly everywhere they exist. But as a corporation, it is more like Coca-Cola than Google."

With 8,500 titles in its catalog, Toei owns more content than any other Japanese firm. Its biggest hits, such as *Sailor Moon* and *Dragon Ball*, receive stellar ratings in the United States and have become household names for generations of American kids. In 2006, the MIP-TV conference at Cannes—the very event where Sandy Frank first encountered *Battle of the Planets* three decades ago—gave its Lifetime Achievement Award to an organization rather than to an individual. The recipient was Toei.

Expectations are high—at least outside of Japan.

But Toei's Nerima headquarters bear nary a trace of the electric energy and futuristic visual feel of the medium that it makes and markets. The headquarters are very clean, with walls bearing beautifully mounted cels from several of Toei's classic titles. A three-foot-high shelf encircles a room containing, in chronological order, a DVD and a VHS copy of every title that Toei has produced.

Down to the old-school feel of the china teacups with which I am served, bearing the company's fifty-year-old Puss 'n' Boots logo, the heavy formal atmosphere feels as though the building has had, to paraphrase Schodt, all the life sucked out of it.

And while the head of the international division, Takazou Morishita, is upbeat on the potential for anime in America, his more defeatist responses to questions about Toei's specific challenges are revealing: "It's tough selling DVDs in the U.S.," he says. "People would rather buy them online. You see, the Americans have made lots of merchandising money [from anime-related products], but we Japanese have not been strong in securing profits from secondary usage. We have done very badly."

However accurate, these are not the sort of complaints one expects to hear from an industry giant in the midst of a global boom. But Morishita's pessimism is echoed in consumer gripes over Toei technical errors, poor production standards, carelessly negotiated or (in the case of *Sailor Moon*) revoked rights, and other sloppiness or insensitivity that are commonly heard in the American otaku community. Despite its past reputation and industry significance (as Miyazaki's and Takahata's first employer, among many other anime firsts), the company seems to be struggling to find its footing in a newly internationalized market in which the rest of the world is now watching, and watching closely.

Toei is not the only producer in the anime industry faltering just as its overseas image and interest is gaining life, nor is anime the only industry facing such challenges. But Toei's size and prominence warrant attention. Lewis points to another lumbering Japanese brand behemoth, Sony, whose most eagerly sought global product in 2006, the PlayStation3, had its release date pushed back by nearly a year because of production delays. In the same way that the iPod transformed Sony from a leader into a follower, CGI, broadband mobile services, OneSeg (the Japanese digital cell phone TV launched in April 2006), and a host of other digital-age innovations have made Toei—one of the most visible and prestigious producers of Japanamerica products—reactive rather than radical.

In June 2006, a few months before Japan's then prime minister Junichiro Koizumi stepped down, the health ministry released a statistic that dominated national headlines: Japan's birthrate had dropped to 1.25, the lowest in its history, and a couple notches below its projected rate of 1.4.

According to demographers, the average birthrate required to keep a population stable is 2.1. The U.S. birthrate is 2.09. Japan's most recent statistic drops it to number 218 on the *CIA World Factbook* national birthrate list—a list that accounts for 226 countries.

"It's an extremely tough figure," the prime minister said.

For the anime and manga industries, as well as for other producers of Japanese popular culture, "extremely tough" may be an understatement. From the hollowing out of its labor force of talented young artists willing to work for years on a meager salary, to the shrinking of its domestic audience, the future for Japanese pop culture just might be in places like America—by necessity.

Various reasons are given for the drop-off in domestic demand, from cell phone advances—enabling younger Japanese to spend hours, and wads of money, each month communicating with one another, watching videos, cruising the Internet, playing games, or just talking, all without ever cracking a manga—to the dearth of quality new manga and anime titles.

But the falling birthrate, falling since 1975, is chief among all factors, and it puts into bold relief the risk that some in the industry took in turning inward and focusing almost exclusively on the domestic market during the 1970s and '80s. Though some of manga and anime's finer artists may have produced the medium's most adventurous works during those years—the works that aficionados like Alt wax nostalgic about when decrying the industry's new global self-consciousness—many of its studios lost valuable time in which they should have developed coherent marketing and distribution plans to meet the needs of a growing international—and fully wired—audience of otaku.

Most studios are now struggling to catch up with a future that is racing ahead of them. A few are attempting to lead the way.

the american way

Masakazu Kubo believes that knowing the American character is what matters most for Japanese producers and publishers. An executive producer at Shogakukan, the Japanese publisher that transformed Nintendo's Pokemon video game into a global multimedia empire, Kubo was there in November 1995, when Nintendo phoned his office and asked if he would cross town and have a look at their new game. He was already an established editor of children's manga at *Koro Koro* comics magazine. Nintendo knew he would get the picture.

Pokemon's immediate success in Japan led the companies involved in its production—Nintendo, Game Freak, Creatures, and

Shogakukan—to set their sights on the United States. "Japan is still the most competitive cartoon market. We knew when we became number one here so quickly, we'd have a chance in the U.S." And making it in the United States usually means making it worldwide.

But Kubo's and others' missteps along the way illustrate his larger point about the future of anime and manga as global products. It's not enough, he says, simply to find a partner in America and let go of the reins. In order to reap the profits they deserve, and appeal to a wider swath of the American population, industry professionals need to acquaint themselves with the particulars of American culture—our business ethics and processes, ethical assumptions, and aesthetic tastes. An anime or manga title may go global through America, but that doesn't mean that America *is* global.

Some degree of localization, Kubo believes, is inevitable. "For example, I tell our people working in the U.S. to localize our work so that it will be funny—and drop any dirty jokes. Japanese people don't really understand what's funny in the U.S. For example, I have no idea why 'Sponge Bob' is funny. But we want the U.S. kids to laugh, and we want their moms to laugh as well."

Twenty years prior to Pokemon, the Tatsunoko brothers simply shipped their product to Sandy Frank at NBC, who then did all the localization on his own, with teams in Los Angeles and New York. "It wasn't cheap, and it wasn't easy," says Frank now.

Kubo advocates a hands-on approach, with Japanese professionals working in tandem with their U.S. counterparts, producing some of the product in the United States—and paying particularly close attention to the nature of American business and legal practices.

He should know.

Pokemon was a Japanese idea exported to the United States. But Shogakukan and its Japanese partners are known in the anime industry for having lost millions to their U.S. distributor, a company called 4Kids.

Kubo's explanation of the 4Kids affair and its recent acrimonious end should serve as a case study, a hard lesson for Japanese anime producers seeking to do future business in the United States. Using a white display board and multicolored magic markers, he literally draws the picture of how it happened.

In famously group-oriented Japan, all four of the aforementioned companies involved in Pokemon's multifaceted creation banded together to handle U.S. rights. Their representative in America was Nintendo America, but their distributor was the New York-based 4Kids, headed by Alfred R. Kahn, a name Kubo utters through slightly clenched teeth.

"Usually, when you think about licensing, you'd think the person who created the original story would make the most money. But American business is designed so that the people at the end, the mass retailers, make the most. Like Wal-Mart. Anything Wal-Mart says, the toy makers do. And they do it for nothing."

The retail/distributor-based American business structure took the Japanese companies by surprise. And the anime industry's emphasis on the creator, artist, or director further blinded them to the actuaries of Pokemon's windfall profits. They knew that there was money coming in, and at the time—partly because of their pride in seeing the Pokemon movie *Mew2 Strikes Back* become Japan's biggest box-office success in America—they were satisfied. Until they learned how much money *should* have been coming in.

"Finally," Kubo says, easing away from the elaborate sketches on the white board, "we understood the U.S. picture. And now we have plans for doing everything differently in the future."

Some of those plans have already been executed in the publishing industry. Kubo erases the squiggles and squares showing the elaborate and inefficient model culminating in 4Kids's dollar signs and draws a much simpler chart, with a new company—Viz Media LLC—at the far end. Viz, based in San Francisco, handles property rights for film, TV and video, the Internet, and publishing products. In July 2006, Viz and the Cartoon Network entered into a collaboration in which they will jointly produce and broadcast anime titles.

His company cannot completely break its ties to 4Kids, Kubo explains, partly because they can't change the voice-over actors now wedded to the title's characters. And what of 4Kids kingpin Kahn? Kubo insists that they're still friends, but "we don't talk business anymore. Not at all."

Kubo's experiences with Americans extend beyond the corporate boardroom. He frequently speaks at anime and manga conventions and American universities, and he reveals an unusually deep knowledge of the American public, for which he has considerable respect. This is especially notable for a man of his age (early fifties) in the anime industry. He combines a veteran's knowledge of domestic production with a global vision of anime's future. Speaking to me in front of shelves stacked high with stuffed Pikachus and other furry characters, Kubo is also warm and charming, making his first career choice—schoolteacher—seem natural, and his actual profession—making characters for kids— entirely apt.

Unlike many others of his generation, he is also unafraid to tackle the future challenges posed by the Internet.

Speaking to a group of students at the University of Nevada in 2005, Kubo decided to turn the tables and ask them a few questions. The students were eager to give the man who'd brought them Pokemon an earful.

What do you find most enjoyable about anime? He asked them, expecting to hear raves about the graphics or storylines. Their response surprised him: the 'fansites,' or web sites run by American otaku.

What Kubo learned taught him volumes about how Japanese producers will need to navigate the Internet in order to have a future of any kind at all. The students told Kubo that they gravitate to Web sites run by anime fans because they are the only places where subtitled anime films are available. The American voice-overs, they said, all sound the same, while the original Japanese versions have far greater range and quality.

"And that's partly our fault, a problem with our business model," he concedes.

The voices for most Japanese anime films are recorded in Canada, where the national government subsidizes the industry.

Canada saves the Japanese producers money. But there are far fewer voice-over actors working on anime in Canada than there are in Japan. The English-language voice of the high-kicking heroine in one anime is likely to be the same as that of the cute schoolgirl in another. Plus, synchronizing the English script with animated mouth movements drawn and designed to speak Japanese poses obvious difficulties.

"The students told me that the Japanese originals are more fun, more entertaining. I understood immediately, and I agreed. But I said, 'Do you know that those are all illegal bootlegs?' And their response was interesting. They said, 'If you make the original DVD with English subtitles, we'll buy it. Or if you make an official site online, we'll sign up and pay for it.' I really believe them. We haven't done that, so they've done it themselves."

Using as a model the *doujinshi* scene, in which official producers support the fan-made unofficial products to ultimately expand the market's scope and impact, Kubo believes that the easiest way around the Internet obstacles of copyright laws and censorship will be to collaborate with the fans who run the fansites.

"Maybe we could license titles to the fansites," he says, his eyebrows rising. "We could then simultaneously release titles in Japan and the U.S., the two hungriest and most impatient markets in the world. Just like they did with *The Matrix*."

To most anime fans, of course, the most infamous copyright breach in the annals of Japanamerica is Disney's *The Lion King*. Again, Kubo's take on the controversy is enlightening: Tezuka Productions, he believes, misunderstood America. If they had not done so, they would have earned the profits, respect, and fame their creator deserved.

"I was told that Tezuka's staff went directly to Disney to complain," he says. "And Disney quite rightly turned around and showed them old manuscripts of Osamu's work. 'Look, here's an imitation of Disney, and here's another one,' they said. So the Tezuka people gave up and went home."

But had the Tezuka Productions staff shown the American media, and by proxy, the American public, the numerous examples of plagiarism, Kubo thinks the story would have turned out differently. "When Kurosawa Productions complained that Disney's 'A Bug's Life' looked a lot like 'The Magnificent Seven,' they did so publicly. And Disney immediately sent a top executive to Japan to deliver a gift and apologize."

Tezuka's staff did not understand America, says Kubo. Future anime producers will have to learn the American way.

"The American public is powerful," he says. "Just being in a fishbowl like Paris Hilton can make you famous, even if you don't do anything. If Tezuka's people had had a better understanding of America, then Osamu himself may have become as famous as Disney."

Kubo folds his hands, looks askance at his white board sketches.

"We were sued so many times over Pokemon in America. Nintendo America had a great team of lawyers, otherwise we wouldn't have survived. But I learned another lesson: In America, if you succeed, you get sued. If nobody is suing you in America, you haven't made it there."

the future trio

Mention the global future of anime to anyone in the know, and three companies are commonly cited: Production IG, producers of *Ghost in the Shell* and collaborators with Quentin Tarantino on the *Kill Bill* films, Studio4C, cutting edge artists with an international bent, and Gonzo Digimation Holding, or GDH.

About five-hundred yards from the tony Park Hyatt hotel featured in *Lost in Translation* are the sleek glass and steel headquarters of Gonzo Digimation Holding (GDH), the youngest of Japan's listed anime studios.

The office of its president, Shinichiro Ishikawa, combines the totems of a teenage boy's bedroom with the icons of information-age commerce. There are plastic models perched atop shelves cluttered with video games, Gundam toys, and comic books. Vivid publicity posters from various anime titles adorn the walls, and a selection of neatly labeled DVDs is stacked near his desk. Pride of place is granted to a large flat-panel PC display, and the youthful-looking thirty-something Ishikawa himself dresses like a Silicon Valley CEO—pressed white shirt, no tie, lean dark suit.

Unlike most of the other anime production headquarters, GDH's look and feel entrepreneurial, wireless, and alive.

The global anime boom has brought listed anime companies onto the radars of major institutional investors who might have ignored the industry only a decade ago. Investors want to know more about the industry's dynamics, and various securities houses have tried to get them the information they want.

According to Mizuho Securities, the contemporary Japanese anime industry comprises four distinct segments, each defined by a different management style and by a different approach to nurturing both talent and overseas growth:

(1) Those that focus on domestic expansion and outsourced production, such as TMS, Sunrise, Shinei Movie, Nippon Animation, Pierrot, and Madhouse.
(2) Those that focus on aggressive overseas expansion and outsourced production, such as Toei and Shogakukan.
(3) Those that focus on domestic expansion and autonomous production—principally, GDH and Studio4C.
(4) Those that aggressively emphasize overseas expansion and focus on autonomous production, such as Production IG and Studio Ghibli.

Although only 23 percent of GDH's total sales currently come from the U.S. market, the figure satisfies Ishikawa—for now. Rare among his colleagues, Ishikawa actually has a long-term strategy for exploiting rising U.S. demand.

In 1996, Ishikawa was at Insead, the global business school in Europe, studying business and mingling with the institution's diverse student population. He had been sent there by the Boston Consulting Group, where he had specialized in technology and new media convergence.

If the late 1990s was the Internet era, ran his reasoning, soon to be followed by the broadband era, then the infrastructure itself would quickly become commoditized. That process would eventually lead to a content era—a period that might, thought Ishikawa, make anyone whose content was specifically tailored to the realities of the digital age very rich.

A group of Israeli and Lebanese friends told Ishikawa that, as a Japanese person seeking to run a content-based business, he had only three options: karaoke, video games, or anime.

"I quickly realized that everyone was singing Madonna, not Japanese songs. Games were a possibility, but I could also see then that the Japanese market was separating, and I was right. The U.S. and European companies became much stronger. In 1996, eight out of the top ten games companies in the world were Japanese. Now it's down to only two or three. So I chose anime."

The field was filled with largely big players then: Disney and Warner Brothers in the United States, Toei in Japan. "Big animation players were old economy," he says. "They were huge organizations run like huge bureaucracies. It was the perfect space for a venture company to enter."

Ishikawa believes that the eventual global failure of Japanese video games serves as a lesson for the Japanese anime industry, especially as it seeks to entertain a new global audience that technology has rendered possibly the most fickle in world history.

"The fundamental problem with Japanese video games companies," he says, "is that their management was very Japanese. They made content for Japan and assumed it would sell in the U.S. and Europe, so they didn't bother to tweak it for those markets. Sometimes the strategy worked, and simply converted westerners to the Japanese way. But in the long term, the plan is flawed."

Ishikawa has good reason to believe that anime can succeed where Japanese games failed. There are enough differences between the industries and their historical contexts to suggest that anime producers can avoid making the same mistakes that destroyed so many software houses.

"With games in the 1980s and '90s, Japan was basically focused on a console market," he says, "while the U.S. and Europe concentrated on the PC. Initially, being close to the hard technology gave Japanese companies an advantage, but that edge was fast chipped away. Microsoft and Electronic Arts were simply cleverer and more aggressive than Japanese companies at globalizing their product."

As others have said, the basic product in anime, the narrative and the artwork, are not wedded to advances in technology. "The anime industry is character driven, and the basic creativity comes from manga. There are still at least ten weekly manga magazines that sell thirty million units per week. On top of that, there are monthly magazines and comic books. In the U.S., the total annual comic market is fifty million units. In the span of one week, Japan does a full year's worth of U.S. comic sales. That's a social infrastructure that has been in place here for three decades, and it means we—the Japanese under fifty—are raised in a culture that has a huge creative advantage. The Japanese power to leverage anime is not a technical thing. The very social structure of Japan is our greatest advantage."

Ishikawa's focus on the creative side of the industry is reminiscent of the description by Steve Alpert from Studio Ghibli of Japan's artist-focused process, and of its pros and cons. But Ishikawa is not suggesting that the artists simply do what they want while the studio prays for genius.

"As a nation of creators, what we have to do with our advantage is make the business more global, rather than just sending our content abroad and making 4Kids and some other American or European companies huge amounts of money."

Ishikawa believes that by revolutionizing the Japanese approach to its future entertainment-related IP, and by turning anime into a major Japanese export, the domestic video game industry could also bounce back. Once Japanese industries accept that they must change, they have a reputation for implementing change swiftly and efficiently.

If online gaming becomes the boom of the broadband era, he says, "I'm certain Japan can be king of games again."

Ishikawa's faith in the potential for localization, for studying the U.S. anime market and, at least to some extent, catering to its tastes, parallels Kubo's emphasis on learning the American mind-set. When I note that some older American otakus, like Alt, feel that the globalization of anime is its downfall, Ishikawa brushes away the complaint.

"Comedy is a good example of something extremely localized. Americans don't truly understand British humor. Look what happened when America made *Mr. Bean*. It was a horrible movie. The Internet has been critical in establishing a sense of globalness, and that is why I went into anime. It is a core competence of Japan that can successfully be globalized."

Ishikawa stayed at the Boston Consulting Group for the first three years after his start-up animation company was founded, farming the management out to friends. In 1999, he discovered that the company was making 10 percent margins on annual revenues of $2 million, so he quit Boston Consulting to run the operation. He would be the brains behind the business, and Shoji Murahama, a former Gainax anime producer of considerable pedigree, would be left to create the magic.

The Macquarie Securities analyst Oliver Cox regards the partnership as central to the emerging success of the GDH model. To remain competitive, Japanese studios need significant capital to invest in digital technology. To make that kind of money, they need to produce quality anime—a prospect that becomes more daunting as Japan's population continues to decline, and as its best talent often seeks out the biggest money—in the U.S. animation industry, in the video game industry, or in other lucrative jobs that did not exist twenty years ago, such as Web site design and online content production.

Ishikawa agrees that anime's most imaginative moments have come when the talent has been left alone to strut its stuff. "But that will only work," he adds, "if the financial side of things is being handled by a serious entrepreneur with a taste for the Wall Street way."

The Mobius strip turns again, though this time with dollar signs stamped onto its sides.

Ishikawa believes that American animation producers like Disney, Warner Brothers, and Hanna Barbera actually created what is now the opportunity for Japanese anime. By restricting their sphere of influence to children between ages two and ten, the U.S. companies never really let animation become a publishing or production phenomenon for anyone else.

"It is not that Japanese cartoons are better than American titles," he says. "It's just that as a cultural platform, they came to influence more people across a broader spectrum of society. It changed their preferences, but also served their wider tastes."

America, he adds with a smile, is now ripe for the future growth of anime.

"I was in Arizona recently. There are a lot of U.S. kids who think that Pokemon is an American word. And maybe it is now. Older viewers can tell it was made in Japan, but little kids can't. Japanese anime has been part of a continuing education in Japaneseness at the TV level."

The demands of a more mature market create additional challenges, many of which are financial. Children care mainly about character, and they usually will tolerate lower, cheaper production values. When companies have an adult audience, they find that they must emphasize quality, which these days means having the capital and the technology to produce CGI materials.

Whereas Tezuka Osamu and other early anime artists worked amid the technical prowess of Disney, Ishikawa sees Pixar as his contemporary rival.

He shows me some publicity shots from one of GDH's 2005 productions: a colorful retelling of the story of the Count of Monte Cristo, but with battle suits and heavy firepower. Its images were exhibited recently at the Grand Palais in Paris's Champs Elysées.

That, Ishikawa explains, was part of an older strategy of trying to make the GDH brand rival Miyazaki's Studio Ghibli. Ghibli is now known worldwide. And at home, a 2005 *Nikkei Shimbun* survey found that Ghibli was the most beloved brand in the land, ahead of Toyota and Sony.

But nobody knows the names of Pokemon's creators. GDH's plan is to go directly into the U.S. and E.U. markets, and to work together with their toy and video game makers.

"Development is not that hard," Ishikawa says, rising from his chair with excitement. "It's exploitation that's more difficult. Grasping the value added, instead of letting 4Kids get all the money."

Ishikawa's plan to work directly with the likes of Hasbro and 4Kids as joint producers of new ideas takes Japanamerica into the future of binational/cross-cultural anime productions.

The U.S. toy maker will come up with the hard product—trading cards, model soldiers—and GDH will make the Japanese-style animation content to go with it. The scheme represents a potential growth spurt for the anime industry, no longer pushing at the door of an entertainment industry dominated by the United States, but joining the American music industry and Hollywood as a participating member of the club.

If the toy concept catches on internationally, Ishikawa says, then the anime can simply be reimported back to Japan, which would be another remarkable innovation, echoing TokyoPop CEO Levy's hope that he can cultivate manga artists in the United States who will eventually reenergize the Japanese scene.

Ishikawa's strategy also involves live action: having anime titles remade with big Hollywood stars and turned into blockbusters.

"We want to be like Marvel Entertainment. Basically, Marvel made two big hits based on cool action comics—*X-Men* and *Spiderman*. Overnight that turned their library of 100 other comic titles into a goldmine. So that's what we want to do. We have a lot of content. If we make one successful U.S. feature film, we are going to be laughing."

That laughter may have already begun.

Ishikawa hands me some snapshots of himself and Samuel L. Jackson wearing traditional Japanese samurai garb during Jackson's trip to Japan in 2005. The actor—who now has otaku credibility because of his role in the most recent *Star Wars* trilogy—was in Japan to do the voice for GDH's *Afro Samurai*, which will be the first Japanese anime to cast a major Hollywood star, and among the first to be made primarily with the U.S. market in mind. It is also a nod to anime's long-standing popularity in the hip-hop community.

"Samuel Jackson is deeply involved in the *Afro Samurai* story," Ishikawa says. "He kind of stole the demo DVD from our agent, and called to say that he wasn't going to give the DVD to anybody else because he liked it so much. Then he asked me to fly to Toronto, where he was filming *I Am the Man*.

"When I arrived, he was shooting a key scene. He had just been shot, so he was lying on the floor. The director yelled 'cut,' and Jackson-san jumped up and marched over to me. In front of the whole cast and crew, he said: 'Don't let anyone else do *Afro Samurai*.'"

Ishikawa pauses, folding his hands behind his head. "You know, if this succeeds, our content library changes from a lump of stone into a diamond."

Both GDH and Production IG have realized that retaining skilled creators and talented staff, training producers, and providing an environment where imagination is given free rein and is provided with the best technology must be the anime industry's biggest priority in the future. Both companies have recently completed IPOs, raising capital for precisely that purpose. The long-term survival of Japan's anime expertise depends on securing a business model that makes the industry attractive to young Japanese, whose financial and creative ambitions far exceed those of their parents' generation.

Ishikawa believes that American investors understand best what anime needs to do. He is now racing against the clock to engineer a situation in which Japanese anime is invested in by serious U.S. money. Silicon Valley / CGI techniques and other expensive technologies are becoming necessary to the future of the animation business, and Japanese studios will need significant capital just to retain their position against future competition.

Just as anime may be Japanizing the way Americans are entertained, the financial realities of the industry may be Americanizing the entire structure of Japanese financial thinking.

American investors have long appreciated the logic of investing in nonmaterial properties, like blockbuster movies, and many have grown rich as a result. Accordingly, Ishikawa wants anime to be the vehicle for introducing a vital concept to the Japanese investment community—the concept that there are spectacular returns to be made on projects whose output is intangible.

If that means cozying up to U.S. investors and forcing Japanese investors to adopt the Hollywood way, he says, so be it.

But will that produce a narrative and visual style dominated by Hollywood sensibilities in the future? How far can partnerships go, before you lose the essence of the art and culture from which the form emerged?

Studio4C's Michael Arias recounts Hollywood's reaction to *The Animatrix* when it was released in the US: "A lot of the people around the Wachowskis, when we'd go to anime and comic conventions together, were looking for stuff that graphically looked like anime, but still had basic American storylines—you know, like the guy with the gun protecting his family and shooting all the enemies. They wanted big tits and cool violence, but not the story lines and genius that define anime."

The danger anime faces in the future, as its Japanese artists and producers return America's embrace, is less financial than artistic: a diluting of its indigenous sensibility when stirred into America's melting pot.

"It's a style of design that looks very new to Americans. But the kind of archetypes they're still looking for in the stories is defined by Hollywood. When we were talking to producers after *The Animatrix*, they were saying—can you do this and this and this in anime?" Arias shakes his head. "It was just a bunch of Hollywood ideas in anime style."

But Hollywood partnerships may not be anime's only option for future growth.

In June 2006, the *Yomiuri Shimbun*, Japan's highest circulation daily newspaper, reported that Japan's largest trading companies were, for the first time, investing in anime series and movies—and deploying their vast international networks to increase anime exports.

For over a century, trading firms like Mitsubishi and Itochu have been the real muscle behind Japan's manufacturing export prowess. While the electronics, cars and semi-conductors eventually sell themselves, the international networks of Japan's major trading companies are invaluable, especially in the early stages, in getting both the word out and the products shipped and distributed.

In early June, Mitsubishi established an $18 million joint fund with Japan's and the world's biggest advertising firm, Dentsu, for investment in Japanese anime, with a plan to finance fifteen to twenty anime features a year and sell broadcast licenses to American television stations. Earlier, Itochu created a joint fund with Time Warner, owners of the Cartoon Network, to invest in the production of new anime titles and accelerate their export to foreign markets.

While Japan's politicians have begun touting the merits of Japan's popular culture at home and abroad, government investment pales next to the involvement of its trading and advertising firms, who have always preferred action to words. Their sudden shift in attitudes signals a sea change in Japanese thinking; their investments and willingness to make use of their vast networks speaks not only for the quality of the products and their potential appeal in America, but also for the notion that Japan is finally prepared to take seriously its intellectual properties, and to sell its ideas.

9
anime appeals

If the Americans Walt Disney and Max Fleischer gave to Tezuka Osamu and to Japan in general a more cinematic style of animation and a template for cute, expressive character design, then the Japanese—as they have done with neon and baseball—took the American import to the next level. Just as neon bathes nearly all of Japan's cities in a dazzling array of colors matched only (and less imaginatively) by our Vegas strip, and just as Japanese baseball fans are as fanatical about the national high school tournament as they are about the pros, animated illustrated characters are a fixture of the nation's daily life.

From the google-eyed, globe-bodied cartoon airplane that greeted me when I first arrived as an adult six years ago at Osaka's Kansai Airport, to the animated cartoon clerks bowing in uniform on my ATM screen, cartoon representations are ubiquitous. They peer down at you from billboards, flash past on the sides of automobiles, gaze longingly through train station mega-crowds, and inhabit your home on packages and mail flyers.

Some are simply advertisements, of course, selling everything from sex shops to Levi's jeans, but others are indicative of the national spirit. *Yuru chara*—from *yurui* characters, or laid-back, soothing, relaxing cartoon icons—are manga mascots used to represent almost every region of Japan, symbols of the identity their local governments wish to project. Sports manga, a genre that has not found an audience in the United States, features special series following the lives of athletes during a given real-life athletic event—Olympic athletes, baseball players during the Japan Series, soccer players amid the World Cup, and so on.

If you live in Japan for an extended period, you're likely to forget that you are constantly confronting cartoon characters—until you leave. When I return to the United States, I am instead confronted by models and movie stars. Real photographs, but are the images more realistic?

"Don't you think this is such a childish culture?" a Japanese friend in her forties once asked me as we walked in Tokyo. "With all these cartoons everywhere?"

Japan has long been a relentlessly visual culture, from its kanji ideographs to *ikebana*. Also, its national faith, Shinto, is both polytheistic and fundamentally animistic—all things, even inani-mate objects, are inhabited by *kami*, spirits or gods—making it easier to understand how a vast building like Kansai Airport might have a cartoon representation, a wide-eyed icon of its attentive and energetic soul. And like the piped-in music and twittering bird songs emitting from speakers along train platforms, outdoor shopping areas, and every other storefront, the various illustrated characters tend to add a softer, more playful atmosphere, or a flash of dreamy imaginative fantasy, to a crowded, urgent, and intensely hard-working urban culture.

When I return to New York, the city's edges feel a lot harder and less forgiving, its signs and billboards more focused and demand-ing. I become grateful for the sounds of steel drums, saxophone, or violin on a dirty and rugged subway platform—sounds that are performed not piped-in, of course, yet serving a similar function.

Childlike sometimes, I replied to my Japanese friend's cartoon critique. Playful, colorful, cute, and sometimes crazy, which I don't mind at all.

It can be as difficult to define why we like certain works of the human imagination as it is to define why we like certain humans—especially before we have ingested too many commen-taries telling us why we are or are not supposed to like them.

For Susan Napier, raised in Cambridge, Massachusetts, as the daughter of two Harvard professors, and now one of the leading anime/manga scholars in the United States, the attraction to anime and manga was near instantaneous—it happened when a student presented her with a copy of the manga *Akira* in the 1980s. Before that, she had been a girlhood fan of the Disney clas-sic *Fantasia*. But anime was a revelation.

"One day a student showed me an edition of *Akira*. I remember opening it to a page with, I think, a single illustration on it—a gigantic black crater with a strange, wizened human being next to it. I had also been a sci-fi fan in middle school, and this pic-ture made me think of apocalyptic science fiction. I was very intrigued—it seemed so sophisticated and imaginative. The next year I was in London when the European premiere of the animated version of *Akira* took place. The British critics were generally quite respectful so I went along and had a look and was bowled over by the intensity, complexity, and grotesque beauty of the film. I had no idea that animation could be like that."

The *Fantasia* connection is no accident. Many fans of pre-Internet animation cite the film, in which Walt Disney tried to elevate animation as an art form to a more sophisticated plane, as an early encounter with the possibilities of the form. According to Ghibli's Steve Alpert, Disney was deeply disappointed by *Fantasia*'s comparative lack of commercial success. "Disney thought it was the future of animation and was crushed by the response. He was working with Salvador Dali on a project called *Destino* [later revamped with CGI in 2003]. He was like, Forget about these little stories we need to make money. Let's do something major. That's where Disney was going with it: the freedom of expression and movement and music without being tied down, which is where the best Japanese stuff is today."

But how does one go from *Fantasia*'s elegant mysticism to Katsuhiro Otomo's nuclear crater in *Akira*?

For Americans, the attraction is not merely aesthetic. Japanese anime and manga are frequently less inhibited and more diverse than American animations, more compelling in their narrative and character developments. Japan's motion picture industry, realizing that it would never match Hollywood's prowess, never fully took flight, so the best and most innovative visual artists took refuge in the underground forms of anime and manga. Film was one of Japan's cultural (and fiscal) backwaters. "Even [the internationally recognized director] Akira Kurosawa was regarded as a hack in Japan until he was recognized in Europe and the U.S.," notes author Matt Alt. "Spielberg, Lucas, and Coppola gave him the money to make *Ran*."

But Alt's insistence on his encounters with early anime titles like *Robotech* as proof of an alternative universe—a universe where the residents actually took elaborate robots and their narratives seriously—is particularly revealing. "We knew these Japanese people were out there," he says, "We just had to find them."

We have always longed to enter other worlds, and our better stories convince us of their existence, from *A Midsummer Night's Dream* to *Alice in Wonderland*, from *Blade Runner* to *Lord of the Rings* to *Star Wars* to *Spirited Away*. But as Patrick Macias suggested earlier, our homespun fantasies have their known, obvious roots: in Hollywood, with the skilled technicians who are featured in behind-the-scenes or cable TV extras at every turn. At least, for us, Japanese narratives come from somewhere else—a somewhere that actually exists, where the rules are genuinely different and where the imagination seems boundless, free to explore the darker terrains of childhood fantasy and—as in so many video games featuring cute-looking animated ammunition—the lighter side of combat.

My own fantasy nation was England. As an adolescent growing up in suburban America, I became infatuated with certain British rock bands, seduced by their lyrical depictions of what seemed to me to be a more densely elusive society—one that, like Japan, had more rigid social boundaries, but also greater room and respect for eccentricity, for oddity and quirkiness. Most American bands at the time seemed to sing only about rock 'n' roll mainstays like automobiles, romance, and sex, or on a slightly higher level, Christian aspirations and the tension between freedom and responsibility. By contrast, British bands sang about the tension between rockers and fashion-conscious cult groups called "mods" (The Who), or about preserving historical landmarks of rural life (The Kinks), or about the absurdity of materialism (The Clash). That the lyrics were not total fantasies, but were fantasies from and about another very real country, cinched my addiction.

From there, I read British novels, plays, poetry, and historical tomes. I had to go to England, and I did as soon as I could, spending an extended stretch as a college student trying to soak it all in, to anglicize myself. Dismissing rational reservations, I loved the accent, the food, the weather of London, and most of the English people I met and befriended—even if they did not fully love me back.

Via anime and manga, American teenagers today are experiencing a similar sense of transcultural longing. It may be the result of sheer irrational exoticism, an infatuation with a somewhere else that is consecrated by the quality of the art itself. It may also reflect dissatisfaction with the homegrown product. Several recent studies have shown that American brand names have dramatically slipped in their cool quotients worldwide. The perceived belligerence of our international policies has not helped. As the journalist Douglas McGray pointed out in his essay on Japan's rising "soft power," Japan has been perfecting the practice of spreading its culture around the world—something the Americans used to do more effectively than anyone else.

America is a relatively young nation. Somewhere along the way we became complacent about our success, and also became somehow tepid about what we were willing to explore through our imaginations. 9/11 may have begun to heat America up again.

"I think it was a combination of growing up in an environment with no culture of its own," says Macias of his love affair with Japan and its popular culture. "And," he pointedly adds, "the failure of American society to come up with something more compelling than *Robotech*."

Nancy Josephson, a vice president at International Creative Management, the American talent agency, tells me that Japan has become her family's vacation place of choice, whether she and her husband want to go or not. "Whenever we have a couple weeks off, that's where Jacob wants to be."

Jacob is a sixteen-year-old manga reader attending Beverly Hills High School in Los Angeles. He speaks to me by telephone from his home. At the moment, he likes *Naruto* and *One Piece*, both from Shonen Jump comics and distributed in the United States by Viz. "I've been studying Japanese since seventh grade," he tells me. "In sixth grade they gave us a sampling of each language. Studying Japanese came first. In my grade, Japanese is surprisingly popular."

About a quarter of the members of his Japanese class are serious readers of manga. Their favorites are *Death Note* and *Bleach*, he says, the latter of which has also been made into an anime.

"I'm definitely into the Japanese stuff," Jacob says, when I ask him about U.S.-based comics. "The artwork is certainly very different. It varies a lot more than American comics do. The perception of American comics is like the musclemen and the costumes and stuff, whereas Japanese manga has such a broad scope of visuals and topics. It really depends on the manga, though. If you find a good manga it will catch your eye and you'll be interested right away. If you find a crap manga, you won't be interested at all."

I ask him what he looks for in the manga that he elects to buy and read. "An interesting plot line and good artwork, and it has to have a distinct theme—either comedy or action or drama. My top three favorite manga are *Love Hina* for comedy, *Death Note* for drama, and *One Piece* for action."

As Jacob speaks, I am trying to remember my own predilections at sixteen. Not having manga titles at the ready back then (Jacob says he can get them easily at "any nearby bookstore"), I can recollect only VHS tapes by favorite directors, novels and short stories, and treasured records. But I cannot imagine myself at sixteen running through the various categories of manga, and having favorite titles in each one. The very specificity of the genres and of their representative titles sounds awfully Japanese to me.

"I've been to Japan twice," Jacob tells me. "It's just really interesting how orderly everything is." And what does he find most appealing about manga? Besides the artwork, he says, "It saves a lot of money. It can be anywhere from [only] eight to ten bucks per volume. Generally, too, it's quick. It takes me only fifteen to thirty minutes to read through one manga title."

Before we hang up, he adds: "I'm also finding Japanese history very interesting as well. Especially the samurai."

Chelsea and Lauren are both fourteen, though Chelsea is a little older, she confides. They have been leafing through manga titles at the Union Square Barnes and Noble outlet in New York City, and I have been discreetly trying to observe them. Evidently I have failed.

"The stories are just more *interesting*," says Chelsea, taking the lead. "They don't have this predictable idea that they're trying to teach you about something. You know, you'll get into trouble for this or that kind of thing. It's just, like, natural stories about crazy stuff that happens."

And the drawings? I ask. "They're good," says Lauren, folding open a page and raising it up to my face. "See?"

Bold and infectious entrepreneurs like GDH's Ishikawa want to release Japanese anime from its insular noose—to partner with Americans and produce something fresh, enduring, and most of all, lucrative.

But isn't Harry Potter successful internationally partly because of his palpable Britishness? Who wants the astute, spectacled English schoolboy to become a Venice Beach surfer, entranced by witches in bikinis?

According to the former Ghibli producer and Studio4C president Eiko Tanaka, the appeal of what we now call anime is intricately tied to culture, to certain aesthetics that cannot be easily imitated or exported.

"Think of it this way," she says. "It's like Pinocchio walking. In America, it's 1, 2, 3, every step is drawn. But here, it's 1—straight to 5. Sudden! We call this a 'ghost,' when we jump from this to that, from frame 1 to 5. Because we don't draw it completely. Japanese anime developed in this very special way. It's not just that we had no money. Japan is always trying to do things faster with fewer resources. It's an aesthetic vision, not just an economical one. We're more efficient."

It is difficult to argue against Japan's efficiency, from its Prius automobiles to its smoothly functioning, low-crime-rate metropolises, from its up-to-the-minute rail systems to its various minigadgets, most of which seem to accomplish the smaller tasks that you had always hoped someone else would think about.

But Tanaka's essential argument has deeper implications. Japan's way of looking at the world, she claims, is not so easy to replicate. Like knowing the boundaries between *tatemae* and *honne*, it is part of a sixth sense of awareness.

"In Japan," she says, "there's a way of looking at the world only through lines—as in the kimono or *torii* [ceremonial gates].

In Europe, they were using light and shadow. So westerners have long been paying more attention to volume than flat spaces. They don't pay that much attention to the lines. We learned how to express shapes and forms and ideas using lines, so it was easier for us to play with forms. Even if we change a shape a bit, it still looks like the same thing. Japanese people know that. But westerners think in terms of light and shadow. If you change the light, everything changes. Japanese people know that no matter how much you change a shape, the elements are still there. It's difficult for other countries that don't have this tradition to imitate it, because no other country thinks this way."

Let us give Tanaka the benefit of the doubt. Japanese anime and manga view the world differently—as Ghibli's Alpert suggested, they are rooted in a tradition of visual perception that is starkly different from most others.

So, I ask Tanaka: If it is so radically different, why would Americans and other westerners suddenly be drawn to it?

Tanaka calmly eases further into her high-backed chair with one fist clenched against her thigh, perfectly theatrical. "Because we borrow the imaginations of the viewers to make it work. We liberate them. They can see and feel the images themselves, by putting themselves inside them."

Because of their limitations, Tanaka suggests, both cultural and financial, Japanese anime and manga were from the very beginning more interactive forms of visual media.

"Japanese expressionism is defined by subtraction," says *Anime Style* editor Hideki Ono. "A pretty or cute girl is drawn with huge eyes down to the eyelashes, and the hair is drawn to the fine details—every strand. But the ear is not shown. They only draw the parts they want. The eyes are big for sensitivity, the breasts are big, but no one wants to see nostrils, so you leave them out."

And the men? "Smooth-skinned and clean, but also very strong. See, the key is finding that balance: The characters are not possible in real life, but maybe they could be possible, if real life were better than it is."

Contrast this with a movie, which carries almost an overload of visual information, signs that we have become all too accustomed to in the Internet age, and can more easily dismiss. But what if a more minimalist representation, a Japanese anime or manga graphic, attuned to our sensitivities and fantasies, gave us exactly, and *only*, what we wanted to perceive?

"Your brain projects in the missing information in 2D anime, which gives your brain pleasure," says Ono. "So hand-drawn characters present a flat-looking scene without certain information, but the viewer's brain fills in the missing elements and feels great joy. It's like being an in-brain character: You're part of the artistry. That's true of the movements as well. Rather than the Disney smooth movements, Japanese TV animation, for example, has the jerkiness that actually appeals and feels more comfortable to the viewer, because the viewer is participating in the creative imagination."

This level of participation, of making and remaking our sense of a chaotic world, might be the essence of anime's appeal. As one video-game-playing junky quoted in the American media said, explaining his preference for an NBA video game over the actual NBA playoffs on TV: "My Kobe [Bryant] passes. The real Kobe doesn't."

"It's really hard to know exactly how much information the brain needs, and how much to leave out, of course," adds Ono. "That's part of the art. Those girls with such huge eyes—does your brain really feel that they exist? The pleasure from Japanese animation comes from the fact that you can feel like they exist. So the viewers actually have to familiarize themselves with this style. The first-time viewer probably can't yet believe that it's a real person there. The cute character will become cute and pretty only when the viewer believes in the character."

Older viewers, in both Japan and America, may find this transference difficult. Unless you're schooled in the interactive world, its outlets, like the Internet, the cell phone, the iPod and the PS2, may seem impenetrable.

But whatever your age, try watching a DVD of *Akira*, or *Jin Roh*, or any Miyazaki film, or Takahata's *Grave of the Fireflies*, without being moved by the plots, or at least taken aback by the literary freedom and sophistication of their worlds. All narrative art has its hits and misses. These titles are hits, and their scope is likely to astonish viewers of any age, any nationality.

reaching out

Aware that they are sitting on a goldmine of titles—70,000 original stories, by most accounts—and desperate for overseas acceptance, anime publishers and producers are finally reaching beyond their borders, even at home.

Akihabara, the Tokyo neighborhood associated with tech and cartoon geeks, is looking more normalized and more easily navigable. One of Japan's most ubiquitous superstores, Yodobashi Camera, opened a several-story outlet near the train station in 2005—making Circuit City and Best Buy look like bodegas. Shortly afterward, a monolithic building filled with restaurants and cafés opened just yards away. Buskers and amateur cosplayers were shooed off the sidewalks.

Shogakukan's Kubo oversees the Tokyo Anime Center, a bland but brightly lit emporium near Akihabara station that houses anime icons in dolls and robot models, lists major companies, and contains an anime studio in which aspiring young artists can create their own works—nearly free of cost. The center was developed in response to America's Siggraph event, highlighting and honoring talented artists in animation, and it is meant both to promote anime to the rest of the world and also to invite anime artists to Japan. Some forty-five Japanese anime companies support the project through contributions and dues. It is, Kubo says, necessary.

"In 2005, a film called '9' won the best story award at Siggraph," he says. "Tim Burton immediately wanted to make it into a movie. But the creator actually wanted to work in Japan. He came directly to me and said he wanted to work for a company I knew here."

But the Japanese industry has been ill prepared to hire foreigners, Kubo says.

"He will probably do fine at places like Pixar. But we had nothing to offer him. That's shameful."

Kubo worked on creating the Tokyo Anime Center precisely to counter Japan's insularity. He wanted to make a portal through which Japanese and foreign artists might meet and produce the next generation of artistic talent, and he gathered together the heads of major companies to fund the center's opening.

Yet, ironically, his reasons for doing so are strikingly old school.

"We want to compete with Pixar and Disney, of course," he says. "But the main goal is to get the kids who are caught up in their little cyberspace worlds to return to the three-dimensional world, to the here and now." He strokes his graying beard and leans forward, making sure I write his comments down.

"We'd like to have today's kids experience the joys of a real conversation."

just a cartoon

In the winter of 2005, I took my sister, in her late twenties, to a showing of Shinji Aramaki's *Appleseed* in Times Square.

Appleseed has the look and feel of the future of anime. At its best, it seamlessly and subtly meshes three-dimensional CGI graphics with anime's trademark two-dimensional drawings, as when its female heroine's boot plunges into a puddle that suddenly splashes at you from the screen. It merges cyberpunk imagery with the narrative layers of a sci-fi epic, and manages to incorporate explorations of political ideology, philosophical conundrums, and even social discrimination—the robots versus the partially human—into a love story, and a wrenching account of childhood trauma.

But it was a crappy New York day, and we thought several times of canceling the commute from the Upper West Side.

I was unusually insistent. My sister had been to Japan only once, fifteen years earlier—and she had hated it. Her leg had been broken and in a cast, it had been the height of summer, and she, like me several years earlier, had had no idea what people around her were saying.

So we went, braving the rains and our lethargy for a visit to Japanamerica.

The crowd at the *Appleseed* showing was not massive, but it was strikingly diverse. I saw black and Hispanic couples, parents with their adolescent children, older and younger male otaku in clubby little groups. A few female-only clans.

Appleseed played. How odd, I thought, to watch such Japanese-styled pop culture imagery and narratives in the heart of my home: New York City. The cyborg scenery seemed out of place in a city of hard bricks and grimy sidewalks. The characters themselves looked absurdly clean-cut, their faces spotless and neat, their features tightly composed—unlike the pronounced shapes of New York's fantastic array of multi-ethnic mugs.

I had first seen the film in a theater in Shibuya, central Tokyo, where everything made sense, where all the seats were filled, and where everyone was resolutely silent. In New York, a few people snickered at the clunkier melodramatic scenes. Someone let out a roar of approval when one of the cooler soundtrack songs geared up.

Otherwise, it was *Appleseed*—7,000 miles away.

Afterward, I was restlessly keen to get my younger sister's reaction. We emerged into the Times Square miasma of lights. She silently shrugged into her jacket while we hailed a cab.

In the darkness as we were heading uptown, she said, "Wow, that was really weird."

What? I said, thinking she was commenting on my geekdom.

"I was sitting there," she said. "And halfway through the film, I started pinching myself. I mean, I was really getting into it, getting emotional and everything."

She recounted the anime flashbacks to the horrifying murder of the heroine's mother, and a particularly heartbreaking scene on a shoreline, in which the heroine grips at the robotic chest of her now half-cyborg lover, who used to be entirely human, and whose life is fading as she embraces him, shouts at him, and holds him hard in the sand.

"But as I was watching, I kept telling myself in the dark: Calm down," my sister said. "Take it easy. It's just a cartoon, okay? It's just a cartoon."

Just a cartoon. You can imagine the Danish artists whose caricatures inflamed Muslims making the same claim. And anyone daring to predict the events of 9/11 would surely have been accused of having paranoid fantasies of cartoonish extremity. Even now, years after the day, the fragmentary images remain mystical, far beyond the reach of naturalism, more spiritually dense than special effects. The scenes of that day are readily available for study on television, DVD, video and the Internet. Yet they still seem more like visions—nightmarish, fantastical and inconclusive.

The animated image has emerged in America's adult imaginations via Japan—but it has also seen its recent growth driven by key American television series, as GDH's Eric Calderon points out. Calderon is a thirty-something Filipino American who worked in MTV's animation department during the Beavis and Butthead years of the '90s, and now serves as GDH's creative director in the company's LA office. He points to three successes on American TV as signposts for the rise of anime: *The Simpsons*, *Beavis and Butthead*, and *South Park*.

"*The Simpsons* was this early American sitcom with these strange, overly simplified yellow creatures, but it was brilliantly written," Calderon says, adding that if it had been a live action feature, it would have been only "moderately successful. But the *Simpsons* characters just pop at you. It's a great lesson in contrasts. Do I choose between *Roseanne* or *The Simpsons*, or any other live action TV drama? It's a cartoon sandwiched between live action shows, and it's the obvious choice."

The success of *The Simpsons* showed that American TV audiences would embrace animation in a prime-time slot, and its combination of up-to-the-minute topicality and split-second wisecracking with a nevertheless loving nuclear family lead to other cartoon invasions of the American psyche.

MTV followed the 2d TV trend in 1993 with the teenage odd couple couch potatoes Beavis and Butthead, whose inveterate loser status and whiplash self-awareness appealed to the snider side of the Nirvana generation. An apparently honest look at teenage vulgarity, its success nevertheless proved that American audiences could become engaged by the most basic graphics—as long as the writing was captivating.

"On paper it looks like the biggest mistake in the world," Calderon says. "Two guys who do nothing sitting in front of their TV, and some of the worst illustrations you've seen. You're basically watching guys watching TV. But suddenly reductive design got accepted as a form of storytelling. *The Simpsons* has a high cell count, moving characters. It's expensive. But *Beavis and Butthead* is very flat two-dimensional abstract design. You only ever see them front and side. Your mind projects what they look like in the moment—just as it does with anime."

Rounding out the trio is *South Park*, with what Calderon calls "those cute paper cutouts" and episodic storylines. "All three series are examples of what Japan has known for forty years," he says. "They've known all along in manga that you could have cute round characters tell a cool story with a sophisticated script." The three American series from the 90s helped accelerate Americans' embrace of Japanese animation. "For me, it is not a jump to go from those shows to Paul Frank [American designer incorporating cartoon graphics into clothing], Takashi Murakami and shojo manga, with a little Pokemon sprinkled in."

The difference is that anime features like *Appleseed*, *Akira*, *Ghost in the Shell* and *Evangelion* are not comedies. They are post-apocalyptic dramas. And they are often very dark.

GDH and others on the forefront of international anime production are venturing into the darkness, betting that audiences worldwide will no longer care whether what they're watching is animated, live action, CGI, or an amalgamation of all three, and will be equally unconcerned over where it came from or who made it, as long as it appeals. Samuel L. Jackson's *Afro Samurai* posits a Jimi Hendrix-looking warrior obsessed with avenging his father's death in a desolate landscape combining elements of a futuristic and feudal Japan. The moody hip hop soundtrack is composed by Wu Tang Clan's the RZA, who declared at 2006's San Diego Comic-Con International that it represents the pinnacle of his music career.

Arthur Smith, head of GDH's London office, has been struggling for five years to coordinate the company's cross-cultural productions, of which *Afro Samurai* is the first of three. Overseeing collaboration between American and Japanese creators brings the two contrasting cultures into bold relief. "I think a European is the only one who has the patience to deal with the Americans and the Japanese," he says, only half joking. "We're [the British] close to America—but being a fiercely independent island nation off the coast of a major continent, and having a long tradition of politeness and etiquette could define Japan. Japan and the U.S. are polar opposites in many ways. Being a Brit can be an advantage."

In Smith's view, whether a given title is considered animation or not will soon no longer matter. The stories, the styles, and the visions of the creators, plus the involvement of major American stars like Jackson and inventive young Japanese writers like *Samurai*'s Takashi ("Bob") Okazaki, will revolutionize the arts and entertainment of the future. "We don't even call our productions animation. Our competition is Tarantino, del Toro, the Wachowski brothers. And those guys all watch our stuff. Del Toro told us he'd literally copied the outfits from one of our shows and put them into his film. We're making this [anime] mainstream."

More than a century ago, Oscar Wilde, attempting to analyze the European obsession with Japanese woodblock prints and exotic aesthetics, wrote that Japan was a "pure invention," that the country and the characters portrayed in the visions of Hokusai and other Japanese artists did not exist.

Wilde was a great admirer of Japanese aesthetics, of the masks and exquisite use of two-dimensional lines, of what Takashi Murakami would later define as "superflat." Indeed, his claim that Japan was entirely a work of the imagination is among the highest compliments from an aesthete who also believed that "all art is quite useless."

Today we live in a world beset by paradoxes. As physical and psychological borders allegedly grow more porous, nationalism and fundamentalism become further entrenched. Information abounds, yet elaborate conspiracies, terrorist cells and shadow governments lurk at the edges of comprehension and awareness.

Photographs, newspapers, video and blogs are a mouse click away, but we suspect secrets and impulsively distrust what we are told.

Amid the otherwise traumatic and contentious world news during the summer of 2006, it was hard to ignore one of the few playful if unexpected and bizarre political scenes: Japan's then prime minister Koizumi posing as Elvis Presley in the Graceland mansion, surrounded by the American icon's widow and daughter, and by George W. and Laura Bush. That Koizumi is essentially an Elvis otaku was well known in Japan. But few expected him to act like one for the world to see.

Photographs and video clips proliferated in the global media and on the Internet. Many Japanese stated their embarrassment at Koizumi's behavior, which they found ill-befitting a head of state. Some of my American friends wrote in alarm: What's he doing acting like that with Bush?

But whether he knew it or not, Koizumi was performing in a manner that dovetails perfectly with Japan's new image overseas. Japan has acquired what it likes of global culture, transformed it with shades and nuances from its own historical experiences, and delivered it back to the world in a slightly different, decidedly Japanese style. From Japan's atomic bombs to America's own Ground Zero, the relationship between the two nations has culminated in a twenty-first century embrace, however awkward, of apparently disparate sensibilities.

"The U.S. has gone through two decades in the span of five years," says GDH's Calderon, trying to describe the post-9/11 shifts in the national psyche. "In the three months after the attack, the entire country went to the 1950s. Instant unification. Independence is bashed down."

But the acceleration continued. In less than two years, America invaded two nations, but the sense of traumatic uncertainty and fear failed to recede; some might argue that it intensified. "Suddenly we jump into the 60s," says Calderon. "We're realizing that we don't want to think in the way of the 50s. We can't afford to. And then there's this quiet reaching out to the independent art world, especially from the young. And at the same time, here's this flow of introverted, introspective, sometimes peaceful, sometimes fantastical, curious, sad little art form coming from Japan. And that's what's happening with anime."

As I have illustrated in these pages, the flow is growing, and is being tapped and replenished. Just as Hokusai and other Japanese artists revolutionized Western art in the nineteenth century, Miyazaki and a roster of iconoclastic Japanese artists, from Takashi and Haruki Murakami to Puffy AmiYumi and Nigo, are giving us new visions and voices in the twenty-first. Japan's "pure" inventions are once again taking us into the future. And through advances in technology and travel, we, unlike Wilde over a century ago, can now be absolutely certain that the country and its people exist.

epilogue

The Mobius strip metaphor I have used in *Japanamerica* to illustrate the interrelated popular cultures of Japan and the United States has proven to be among its most useful. Since the book's publication, bookstore and lecture hall audiences, journalists and social critics, professors and students, *otaku* fanatics and interested readers alike have embraced the image as a way of understanding a bicultural relationship of increasing intimacy and mutual awareness. And if you can imagine the strip in motion—whirling through the winds of the Pacific and DSL, cable, and satellite TV signals, criss-crossing the fifty states and beyond—you will get a clearer picture of what is happening now: It is tying the two countries even closer together.

The father of anime and manga, Osamu Tezuka, idolized and imitated American artists Walt Disney and Max Fleischer some sixty years ago. Today, as I write, the first major exhibition of Tezuka's protean illustrations is on display at San Francisco's Asian Art Museum—installed simultaneously with an exhibit of master Taisho Yoshimoto's Edo- and Meiji-era *ukiyoe* woodblock prints just down the hall. So-called high and low Japanese arts are colliding under one American roof, and Tezuka, long considered a genius and cultural icon in Japan, is suddenly and finally making headlines in a country whose artists first inspired him, and whose bombs helped shape his dedication to peace.

Three hundred and fifty or so miles to the south, in the heart of Los Angeles, the crack animators and computer graphics artists of Imagi Animation Studios International, with offices in Los Angeles, Tokyo, and Hong Kong, are crafting a feature-length film of *Astro Boy*, Tezuka's signature creation, for release in American and Japanese cinemas in 2009. They are working directly with Tezuka's posthumous studio, Tezuka Productions, whose chief spokesperson, Yoshihiro Shimizu, is directly involved in the project—and who graces *Japanamerica*'s pages with his insights and reflections.

The very same studio, Imagi, is hard at work on another American feature film, *Gatchaman*—the very title that kicks off *Japanamerica* via an interview with Sandy Frank, the NBC producer who brought anime to America in the late 1970s when he purchased and radically redrafted *Gatchaman* into the now retro-classic, *Battle of the Planets*. Imagi plans to release *Gatchaman* in 2008. A sign of the Mobius

227

strip: They will not title their film *Battle of the Planets*. They will use the original Japanese title, *Gatchaman*, because that is what it is called, and that is what Americans want today—the original Japan, raw, unfiltered, unaltered, unhyped.

The number of cross-cultural projects currently afoot is hard to account for, and probably silly in the relatively monolithic form of a book. Blogs are better suited, but it's worth mentioning the Steven Spielberg/Michael Bay version of *Transformers*, based on Japan's Takara toys and subsequent anime series; the Wachowski Brothers' (creators of the anime-homage *Matrix* films) version of *Speed Racer*, to which both Christina Ricci and Susan Sarandon have committed, which was based on the manga and TV series *Mach Go Go*, created by the Yoshida brothers (who also gave us *Gatchaman* in the 1960s), and clips of which were excerpted in the 2005 Geico TV ad campaign; and *Titanic* titan James Cameron's *Battle Angel*, due in 2009 and based on the manga series *Battle Angel Alita*, created by Yukito Kishiro in 1991.

This last vote of approval from Cameron has transformed the relationship between Hollywood and anime/manga, according to Yoko Hayashi, president and founder of Artwoods, a company devoted to connecting Tinseltown with Tokyo. Her partner in Los Angeles was responsible for turning Mr. Titanic into a manga maven, and Hayashi is hoping more such transformations are in store.

"The Cameron decision was a big thing for Hollywood," she says. "If Cameron was pleased, Hollywood producers thought, then we all suddenly want manga. And when they learn that manga are already a big hit in international markets, they become even more enthusiastic."

But not everything in Japan can be exported so successfully—partly because of conditions in both countries. Trans-cultural titles such as *Afro Samurai* and *Tekkon Kinkreet*, whose creative evolutions are chronicled in this book, had mixed critical and commercial receptions, both in the United States and in Japan. Americans—particularly older generations—remain wary of foreign-looking images, whether animated or live action, and their general assumption that "cartoons are for kids" is tough to crack.

"The big challenge is turning a great manga, which is essentially a beautiful and very detailed illustration, into live action," Hayashi says, noting that it's the integration of superior art, design, and story-telling that makes the manga. "But in America," she adds, "live action is what makes money."

Cameron is attempting to circumvent this obstacle via technology. While his *Battle Angel* will technically be a live action movie, it will be shot using a combination of computer graphic animation and three-dimensional film technologies developed by Cameron—who is banking on the existence of a thousand theaters across North America equipped with 3D digital projectors capable of actually showing *Battle Angel* upon its release in the summer of 2009.

Titanic, indeed.

Harnessing intellectual property is a problem for anyone in the creative or content-producing industries worldwide, but as I describe in these pages, the challenge is particularly vexing for Japan's producers of popular culture, who possess neither the resources nor the where-withal to even begin to tackle it. The dazzlingly incestuous relationship of creative exchange between the *doujinshi*, or fan artists, and professionals has helped cultivate wave upon wave of fresh new art, while leaving most in the industry virtually clueless about copyright law.

As one young Japanese reader, upon finishing the book, told me: "I think the reason we can't protect our intellectual property in places like Asia or the U.S. is that we never really did it at home. We don't even understand *how* to do it."

The Internet only exacerbates the scenario. YouTube, the video-sharing site that is now as commonplace as cable TV, came into being while I was conducting research and interviews in 2005. Today, if you type the letters "AMV" into its search box, you will discover thousands of so-called "Anime Music Videos," consisting of a fan's favorite anime clips re-edited and woven together, then set to a soundtrack that is usually a favorite hip hop or pop song of the day. Add that to the legions of fan sites offering streaming and/or down-loadable anime videos, often subtitled by the sites' owners, and the "scanlations," scanned texts of complete manga titles, and you have a global *doujinshi* phenomenon—without a yen of profit.

Inside Japan, concerns about the nation's youth are keen enough to prompt a member of the government's Ministry of Foreign Affairs to use the word "crisis" over an otherwise leisurely lunch with me near his office. The rise of creative competitors in Asia, particularly China, has motivated ministry officials to establish manga awards programs and international youth exchange initiatives under the unlikely rubric "manga diplomacy," all in an effort to keep the focus on Japan—and to light a spark under what many feel is a pathologically apathetic, conservative, and pessimistic younger generation.

"They don't seem to have much hope," says veteran professor, translator, and author Motoyuki Shibata of his students at the University of Tokyo, one of Japan's most prestigious and best-known academic institutions. His current classes contain what he calls "the first generation in modern Japan to grow up without the sense that things would get better."

The list of social ills currently haunting headlines at home and overseas would seem to support Shibata's claims: an aging population and a declining or stagnant birthrate; an expanding class of young, part-time workers (*freeters*) with checkered resumes and scant skills; and so-called NEETs ("Not in Employment, Education or Training"), with their CVs and skill sets suspended in mid-youth. Stories of *hikikomori*, pathological young shut-ins who withdraw into their bedrooms and virtual worlds to avoid the real one; and Internet suicide pacts—through which young loners meet one another online in order to kill themselves together in the bricks-and-mortar world—have become common fodder for domestic and foreign media. "They know they want what they want," explains Duke University Professor Anne Allison, author of *Millenial Monsters: Japanese Toys and the Global Imagination*, speaking of Japan's current crop of liberated but lethargic kids. "The problem is: they're not sure what they want."

The hollowing out of domestic talent described earlier in this book has put many of Japan's pop industries into turmoil—just as Americans are learning how to appreciate their products—and many in the anime business, such as Tezuka Productions, are resorting to outsourcing, further worsening the problem at home.

"Even though demand for animated films continues to rise," says Michael Arias, the Japan-based American director of *Tekkon Kinkreet*, "at home and outside of Japan, anime remains a business that needs to nurture and protect its talent. Making *Tekkon*, I was fortunate to work with some of the best talents in Japan, and I heard over and over from the veterans how depleted the ranks have become in the last ten years, as more of the artists with animator potential pursue work in computer graphics, web design, and other 21st century fields."

"Young people don't have the perseverance anymore," adds Hayashi. "They're such good boys and girls, but they're not hungry. They're content."

And so a final note of irony: The challenge to the industry in Japan is finding enough young people willing and able to create and export Japan's products of popular culture, while the challenge in America is creating an audience that will continue to consume those products as it ages.

Carl Horn, a veteran editor of manga in America currently at Dark Horse Comics, a twenty-year-old U.S. publisher, is optimistic that the current generation of American fans will "age up," in the words of TokyoPop's Stuart Levy, and continue to provide demand for the medium in their later years. The recent explosions in manga's popularity happened, he notes, "at the same time U.S. publishers embraced, rather than attempted to change or conceal, the native differences between Japanese and U.S. comics." Horn believes that America's larger and expanding population, younger median age, public library system (American librarians have largely supported the arrival of manga titles that have helped draw kids back to their shelves), and diversity—providing a greater chance for a variety of narrative genres to appeal to America's subcultures and ethnic enclaves—all point to enormous potential opportunities.

The Anime Companion author Gilles Poitras, whose series of educational guidebooks targets parents and their children, agrees with Horn, pointing to the fiscal need (and possible payoffs) in cultivating an audience that appreciates manga and anime into adulthood. Younger fans don't have the same amounts of disposable income held by their elders, notes Poitras. Even as anime's popularity has bloomed among the U.S. teen and twenty-something demographics, "the amount of money spent per fan has dropped," he says, "and they don't spend as much as anime-obsessed adults do. At least I hope they don't."

Still, unlike their counterparts across the Pacific, American youth do seem hungry for illustrations and animations currently inspiring their imaginations courtesy of Japan. Since the publication of *Japanamerica*, I have received several requests for information from adult American readers whose nephews or nieces, neighbors' kids or their own sons and daughters were bitten by the anime/manga bug, have begun studying Japanese and hope to live and attend universities in the land that produced Tezuka, Miyazaki, and Pokemon. The kids I met on my U.S. book tour possessed such a deep and through knowledge of the various subgenres and arcane titles that I often found myself encouraging them to pen books of their own.

"Young people are now seeking out niches," says Steve Alpert of Miyazaki's *Studio Ghibli*. "In a way that's a good sign, because it requires effort, thinking, evaluation. And maybe it will lead them to appreciate the differences" between the attitudes, ideas, and aesthetics that constitute the two sides of the Mobius strip. Author and professor Susan Napier proposes that this appreciation and embrace of otherness "could be Japanese pop culture's most important legacy."

A twenty-year-old American student currently enrolled in the University of Tokyo's Department of International Studies tells me she is learning "everything I can about this country—the history, the people, the language and the arts. I want to learn it all." She doesn't have much time to talk to me because of her soon-to-start *Aikido* lessons, teachings of a traditional Japanese martial art that combines philosophy and spirituality with physical techniques.

She has bypassed the Internet and flown across the seas to pursue her hunger for Japan to its very shores. But why? I ask. What first inspired her to travel so far from home?

"*Dragonball Z.*"

And maybe that's the ultimate truth of this book. We might appreciate the differences. We might get closer to the world.

Roland Kelts
Tokyo, 2007

index

233